The Ultimate Test

THE ASHES
2009

The Ultimate Test

THE ASHES 2009

Gideon Haigh

First published in Great Britain
2009 by Aurum Press Ltd
7 Greenland Street
London NW1 0ND
www.aurumpress.co.uk

A catalogue record for this book is available from the British Library.

ISBN 978 1 84513 449 5
10 9 8 7 6 5 4 3 2 1
2013 2012 2011 2010 2009

Text design by Alice Graphics
Typeset by J&M Typesetting
Picture section designed by David Fletcher Welch
Printed by MPG Books, Bodmin, Cornwall

Contents

Introduction   ix

Part I—Before the Game   1
Don't Panic   2
Interesting Times   6
Business as Usual   10
Farewell the Strong Man   13
The Shock of the New   18
New Kids on the Blockhole   21
Come Again?   25
Carpe Diem   27
Best of Breed   31
Excess Baggage   34
The Team that Plays Together   37
BC/AD   41
A New Angle   43
Battle Renewed   46

Part II—First Test   51
Day 1   52
Day 2   56
Day 3   60
True Believer   64
Day 4   67
Day 5   71

Sophia's Choice   75
Drawn and Quartered   79
Australia's Overachievers   82

Part III—Second Test   **85**
Going, Going …   86
Day 1   89
Blow-out   92
Day 2   95
Day 3   99
Day 4   102
Day 5   106
Three and a Half Men   109
The Eleventh Hour   111
The Spirit Made Flesh   113
We Need to Talk About Kevin   117

Part IV—Third Test   **119**
Pitch 4U   120
Short Change   122
Birmingham Fault   124
Day 1   126
Unnatural Selection   131
Day 2   135
Losing It   138
Day 3   142
Day 4   144
Day 5   149
Atlas Shrugs   153

Best of Five   156
Short Rations   158

Part V—Fourth Test   **161**
Too Many to Mention   162
Terrace Housing   165
Day 1   167
The Disciplinarian   171
Day 2   175
Kiss Ass   179
Day 3   180
We're All Doomed   182
The Past Is Not Another Country   185
A Room with a View   188

Part VI—Fifth Test   **191**
The Comeback Kid?   192
Meet the New Boss   193
Losing the Thread   194
A House Divided   198
The Fix Isn't In—Yet   200
A Delicate Balance   201
Day 1   205
Day 2   209
Marathon Men   214
Day 3   218
Pitched Battle   222
Over It, Moonwise   224
Day 4   225

The Disappointed   228
The Light on the Hill   230
TINA   233
Consistent Inconsistency   236
The Daily Moan   239
Going Down   242

Scorecards   245
Averages   263
Length and distance conversions   267

Introduction

Ricky Ponting's Australians came to England in 2009 with a variety of missions. Of these, defending the Ashes they had recaptured at home in 2006–07 was merely the most obvious; there were several subsidiary purposes, including defending their status as the world's number one Test nation from the rival claim of South Africa, and ratifying the pre-eminence of Test cricket in the face of the resistless tide of Twenty20. This last priority was subtly re-emphasised by the withdrawal of Ponting and his fellows from the Indian Premier League, and the team's brief and forgettable participation in the World Twenty20: this was a team with eyes on the one prize alone.

Andrew Strauss's Englishmen hosted with a similar sense of priorities, with the incentive that their opponents were not one of the great Australian teams of yore, and that it was only four years since the nation had been sent into transports of delight by the achievements of Michael Vaughan, Andrew Flintoff and Kevin Pietersen. Since then, however, cricket had vanished from terrestrial free-to-air television. This would be a series for the faithful, needing something extra special to attract converts.

Me, I arrived to do something almost unpardonably luxurious: report a five-Test series. The Ashes was the first of its kind; it is the last one left. It's a purist's enchantment and a marketer's nightmare: twenty-five days of cricket which might, as in 1926 and 1953, feature an actual result on only one. It is still, at least where Australian and English cricketers are concerned, the forum that counts. In the main, anyway; nothing can be taken for granted in this fast-evolving, expanding and fragmenting game.

What did I think in advance? We all tend to overestimate the evidence of our own eyes. I'd watched Australia play one of the best summers of Test cricket I can remember, losing 2–1 at home to South Africa, then reversing that scoreline on the reciprocal visit. They were a weaker team than their countrymen were accustomed to, and terribly ordinary at times, but I liked their spirit, and I admired their captain's resolve. His first tour, in 1995, had coincided with Australia's defining recapture of the Worrell Trophy, an initial step in the establishment of their global cricket hegemony; that being so, his whole career had been spent, as it were, on top. He was bearing the setbacks now with humility and dignity, scrapping hard with limited resources.

The English media had watched their team lose narrowly in the Caribbean, then at home beat out of sight a disgruntled and uninterested West Indies. They were optimistic, and not without reason. Dropped into the captaincy, Strauss had fitted like a penny into a slot. In Ravi Bopara, they had a Test batsman of great promise; in Paul Collingwood, they had a tigerish fighter. Pietersen and Flintoff, of course, were 2005 incarnate. Of England's recent exploits, however, I had merely read reports and seen only highlights. Nor could I imagine Flintoff playing all five Tests, and my recollections of James Anderson, Steve Harmison and Monty Panesar from 2006–07 had left me wondering how much they could conceivably have improved between times.

What transpired over the next two months was an exhaustive and exhausting interrogation of the capabilities of two good, ordinary cricket teams with, I suspect, more violent swings in ascendancy than I can remember in my lifetime's cricket watching. Total domination and abject submission was the tenor of Ashes cricket during the 1990s, but the roles were fixed. Here the teams took it in turns, partly because of the conditions, a little because of the umpiring, but mainly because of their accumulation of frailties. Occasionally, it was brilliant; once in a while, it was ordinary; usually, it was fascinating. Sometimes I speculated accurately; often I was wrong, as you can here read for yourself. Like *Ashes 2005* and *Downed Under*, this book is a faithful daily record of my impressions of the series, chosen from words I wrote for *Business Spectator* (Melbourne), *The Times* (London), *The National* (Abu Dhabi), a blog and a diary I maintained for *Wisden Cricketer*, plus some features for *Ladbroke's* and columns for *The Australian* and the *Sunday Age*. The articles are precisely contemporaneous; on two or three occasions, I have combined two pieces into one. The contents date back to reports I wrote for the *Guardian*, *Wisden* and Cricinfo of Australia's summer, beginning at their lowest ebb, as they lost their first series at home to South Africa, and distant impressions of England's winter, in particular the ousting as captain of Pietersen and the sacking as coach of Peter Moores. They end on 24 August, the day after England officially regained the Ashes.

The Ashes still feels like a tour rather than a trip, and my wife Charlotte and I were in a constant state of heartfelt gratitude for the hospitality we received from, among others, Stephanie Bunbury, Michael Atherton and Isabella de Caires, Sophie and Arun Matta, Andrew, Heather, Jenny and Lucy Hutchinson, Norm and Adele Geras, Professor Ken Smith, Susan Johnson, Stephen and Prudence Fay, Simon Rae and Ian Smith. To Michael, I feel a special debt, for it was thanks to his good offices that I found a friendly home at *The Times*. Above all, though, I dedicate this book to Charlotte, who shared her honeymoon with cricket, as she cheerfully shares her life.

Part I

BEFORE THE GAME

Don't Panic

At intervals during the Second Test, the Melbourne Cricket Ground public address system carried a soothing message: 'In the unlikely event of an emergency, the emergency management plan will swing into action.' As South Africa cruised to its first series victory in Australia, fans waited in vain for similar reassurance from their exalted cricket team.

The expectation was pardonable. Since Test cricket's inception at this ground 131 years ago, Australia had only lost home series to England, the West Indies and once to New Zealand. Now they have been beaten out of sight in two Test matches they had the winning of, just a month after their trouncing in India—enough to jeopardise their mantle as the world's number one, and to warm the Ashes just a little.

Australia's defeats in Perth and Melbourne have been two of their gravest, as notable for their manner as their margins. The Australian team of two years ago would have won the Test at the WACA by 200 runs, but South Africa cruised to the fourth-innings target of 414 at a smooth-sailing 3.5 runs an over.

At times in Melbourne, in fact, Ricky Ponting's men played as other countries used to play against them, with a kind of grim, orderly, persevering mediocrity. It wasn't merely because the great man died on its eve that the drama seemed Pinteresque—nothing was quite as it seemed, you spent a lot of time wondering what on earth was going on, and the third day featured a pause in the Australian effort that was no less pregnant for lasting virtually two sessions. The plot, meanwhile, turned expectation on its head. At stumps on day two, South Africa were less than halfway to first-innings parity with Australia, holding just three insecure wickets in reserve. Then a tail that had self-destructed in barely an hour in Perth clung for more than 100 overs. Ricky Ponting, apparently waiting for the innings to perish of natural causes, watched JP Duminy and Dale Steyn preserve their vital spark for 180 runs. Bowlers went through the motions to defensive fields, while catches were spilled and overthrows and penalty runs casually conceded.

Ponting provided a three-act drama on his own. Dropped on 24 at third slip on the first day by Neil McKenzie, who had taken position just the ball before, Ponting hit a scintillating 101 from 126 balls, only to fall to a bat-pad catch on the stroke of tea, playing the interval rather than the ball. On the fourth day, Australia's captain sweated and toiled for more than four hours over 99, but could find no support worth the name. Among his teammates, one spasm of misplaced aggression followed another, with an apparent hankering for the bravado of yesteryear, as though one booming drive through the covers would turn the clock back. The clock passed its own judgement: the entire XI could not last as long as South Africa's last three pairs.

With the ball, Steyn took advantage of Australian batsmen preoccupied with their own private dilemmas. Hayden went into the Melbourne Test talking up how 'awesome' it was to be under pressure personally and collectively, as if cast in a cliffhanger of his own making. The plot, though, was too convoluted: he looked as confused while batting as during the first four Tests of the Ashes of 2005, and suggested none of the deep-buried professional pride that then stirred from him that hard-bitten hundred at The Oval. A month ago, a fourth Ashes tour seemed inevitable; now more people are noticing that his Test average in England is 34.5.

Andrew Symonds, who at his best bends the knee to no bowler, is presently having trouble bending the knee at all. Here he looked ready for a dreadlock holiday, bowling innocuously, flailing miserably at the crease and hobbling visibly in the field. Michael Hussey, who has drifted into bad form as a good man might drift into bad company, nicked one he was trying to leave then didn't nick one he was adjudged to have edged; his average has deflated like a sub-prime asset book, from 86 two years ago to less than 60. Michael Clarke, Simon Katich and Brad Haddin all went too hard at unprepossessing deliveries. Nathan Hauritz walked after a slip catch in the first innings that appeared to bounce but which third umpire Bruce Oxenford seemed unable to resolve—the pause, as in Pinter, finally becoming too agonising.

Defeat doesn't mark the end of an era. The era had already ended. And the thirteen-year green and golden age in international cricket has really been a sequence of overlapping phases, subtly different, distinguished by key retirements: Taylor and Healy in 1999; the Waughs in 2003; Warne and McGrath in 2007. A new era in Australian cricket has so far failed to begin, and the players whom it was assumed would tide the team over in transition have fallen from their high estate.

While no beaten team can be wholly happy, there were hints in Melbourne of unaccustomed buck-passing. Vice-captain Michael Clarke was twice asked at his press conference about bowling choices; twice he admitted not understanding their rationale, and referred the questions to 'the skip'. For his own part, 'the skip' hemmed and hawed over questions about selection, and finally referred his interlocutors to the selectors themselves. Yet the selectors have made only forced changes for the Sydney Test beginning Saturday: uncapped all-rounder Andrew McDonald and pace bowlers Ben Hilfenhaus and Doug Bollinger have been promoted on the basis of their Sheffield Shield form. Injuries defer harder choices.

The Australian malaise is deep enough for some to have envisioned the ultimate in-case-of-emergency-break-glass option: a comeback by Shane Warne to assume the captaincy for the Ashes. A guest commentator for Channel 9 in Melbourne, the Sinatra of spin was conspicuous by his charisma. When the national anthem was performed on Boxing Day by Eddie Perfect, spiky-blond star of *Shane*

Warne: The Musical, there briefly seemed almost no limits to the great man's accomplishments. For the moment, it is a notion more appealing than realistic. Ponting in his most recent tour diary professes not even to have pondered retirement, and it is doubtful he would accept the loss of caste involved in welcoming a new leader. Yet the schedule Australia faces over the next six months will sternly test his vulnerable back and wrist. It will also reveal if anyone actually does have an emergency management plan.

2 JANUARY 2009
SOUTH AFRICA IN AUSTRALIA

Interesting Times

'Boring, boring,' commenced a chant in the lower deck of the Olympic Stand on the third afternoon of Australia's Melbourne Test against South Africa. 'Boring, boring ...'

It wasn't surprising—at that stage only one wicket had been taken that day. Yet no sooner had it begun than it ceased—nobody was joining in. And, in fact, for all the ease with which JP Duminy and Dale Steyn were picking Australia's attack off, this was *interesting*. This, you sensed people thinking, must be the 'cycle' that older fans have been banging on about all this time. Hmmm. Weird.

New sensation it certainly is. To have even a vestigial memory of a time when their country was not the benchmark in international cricket, an Australian must be at least twenty. Melbourne Tests of the last two decades have regularly resembled ritual sacrifices, Australia's fifteen victories accruing by an aggregate margin of 1678 runs and sixty-eight wickets.

The South African surge, too, seems to have burst from nowhere. The average Australian fan is not nearly so well informed about overseas cricket as, say, the average Indian—mainly because it has hardly mattered. South Africa arrived here a good deal more softly than in 2001–02 and 2005–06, when predictions of a stern contest proved dismayingly off-beam. But Graeme Smith, who let his talk do the cricketing here three years ago, has been stunningly recast: with no Warnie to be the butt of, he suddenly looks a substantial figure indeed.

For Australian cricket, as distinct from the Australian cricket team, defeat is not all bad tidings. Reinventing the narrative of Australian success has proven a challenge to the game's marketers. The eagerly awaited Ashes of 2006–07 turned out to be a chore; the backlash against the Australians after the Sydney Test a year ago revealed a core of supporters to have been alienated by the perceived arrogance of their national representatives. At least for a period, defeat might endear Ponting's men to as many fans as it disappoints.

Even the age-old gripe that it is harder to get out of the Australian XI than in might need revisiting. The boys of baggy green represent their country's longest-running TV soap opera, but for some time theirs has been a series in search of new characters. A few have auditioned unsuccessfully, notably the South Australian pair Dan Cullen and Mark

Cosgrove; some might come again, like the West Australian batsmen Shaun Marsh and Adam Voges; more will shortly have their chance, doubtless including 20-year-old opener Phil Hughes from New South Wales, with his keen eye and cast-iron concentration. It's fun to be debating the composition of the Australian team again after so long either scrutinising their etiquette or goggling at their earning capacity.

The Australian press is not quite so innocently amused. Condemnations after the Melbourne Test were crushing, consensuses being easy to build when one man, Rupert Murdoch, controls two-thirds of the daily print media and a single know-nothing comment piece can be syndicated round the country. Australian players still being something of a protected species, criticism has been heaped at the door of the selectors, chairman Andrew Hilditch in particular. News Ltd tabloids even grew all nostalgic for Hilditch's predecessor Trevor Hohns, that 'uncompromising man who made tough decisions'—overlooking how they pilloried Hohns for many of those tough decisions, including demanding his head when Steve Waugh was dropped as Australia's one-day pilot.

The curious aspect of both the Perth and Melbourne Tests, however, was not that Australia lost, but that they lost from winning positions, which suggests that it is not the raw talent at fault so much as its deployment. The figure who has so far gotten off lightest is coach Tim Nielsen, who has between times even had his contract extended to 2011. Perhaps the luckiest figure around, meanwhile, is John Buchanan, who, with timing worthy of Warren Buffett, exited at the exact zenith of Australia's fortunes, the 2007 World Cup.

Speaking of market timing, Australia's is not good. Fans will always regroup and commentators always rant, but sponsors are skittish: hardly a day goes by without some story in the sports pages about a backer backing out, an advertiser reducing exposure or even a broadcaster having second thoughts. And Cricket Australia is renegotiating deals with two of its three platinum partners, Commonwealth Bank and the telco Hutchison, right now.

Watching cricket on television in Australia is a disarmingly seamless experience, so often do the advertisements feature the self-same players. One minute you are watching Adam Gilchrist drive a ball. Next minute he's driving a car. And while Australia might be losing the cricket this summer, they continue dominating the commercials, with Ponting, Hayden, Symonds, Clarke, Johnson and Hussey in outstanding form.

Except that as each wicket fell during Australia's melancholy procession on the fourth day in Melbourne, the jokey ads for everything from financial services to fried chicken began to jar. 'That's stumps!' said Symonds in a corny car ad seemingly at the end of every over; if only it were, said his on-field deportment. For the last fifteen years, Australian players have been chased by advertisers as the Beatles were once chased by screaming teeny-boppers. But if fans in Australia are more loyal than they're sometimes given credit for, corporates are more fickle than they pretend, especially at a time when sponsorship has become very much a buyer's market. It mightn't be long before cosy old boredom begins looking quite attractive.

9 JANUARY
PIETERSEN v MOORES

Business as Usual

For years, English cricketers have obsessed over that myste-
rious dark art of their Australian rivals defined by Steve Waugh
as 'mental disintegration'. At last they seem to have mastered
it—except in one crucial respect. They've forgotten that you're
meant to apply it to your opponents rather than yourselves.

Last month, England's Ashes stocks were high, as
Australia twice squandered winning positions against South
Africa. Now England seems intent on squandering that
squandering, its dressing room as at odds with itself as a
couplet by William McGonagall.

With the Ashes six months away, the series already looms
as a competition between two teams so consumed with their
own weaknesses that their opposition's weaknesses are a
secondary consideration. Yet Australia's challenges are at
least identifiable and familiar: they have simply been beaten,
in two of their last three series, by better cricket teams.
England's problems seem more pervasive, systemic and elusive,
arising mainly from a cricketer in Kevin Pietersen whose ability
first loomed as a solution and whose inability to tolerate a
coach in Peter Moores without an illustrious playing career
has resulted in them both being fired.

Ricky Ponting's Australians are in an incomplete transition; so much cricket awaits them that the team could easily

have undergone another complete makeover by July. In the near term, three away Tests against Graeme Smith's effective and efficient South Africans offer them little to gain, much to lose. The player being scrutinised most minutely is Matthew Hayden, who used to bring his bat to the middle like Jeremy Clarkson taking a high-performance car for a spin, but who now seems capable only of either idling or running red lights. Omission from Australia's short-form teams is a mercy for him; it probably slightly enhances his hopes of that fourth Ashes tour he would dearly love to make. At thirty-seven, though, he might well have used up his career allotment of comebacks.

Where Australia's bowling attack in Sydney two years ago spoke for more than 1500 Test wickets, in the Test this week it aggregated barely 100. Ponting, however, has one advantage. His low-key coach, Tim Nielsen, was appointed with the captain's priorities and personality in mind, after a period as John Buchanan's deputy then as manager of Cricket Australia's Brisbane Centre of Excellence. Kevin Pietersen obviously fancied the same unilateral discretion, but had neither the support nor the finesse to obtain it.

Before the Sydney Test two years ago, Buchanan vouchsafed that Pietersen 'always seemed distanced from the group' of his fellow players: 'He certainly talks of himself as a team player, but I don't personally see any evidence of that.' Pietersen countered that he was a 'massive team player', offering as evidence batting tips that he had been giving to Monty Panesar—not, perhaps, the most obvious proof available of team-playing massivity.

Nonetheless, there is some sympathy for Pietersen in Australia, given the pretty low esteem in which English coaches are held. The old story is of the English boy told to change his grip by his English public schoolmaster.

'But, sir,' protests the boy, 'this is the way Bradman held it, sir.'

The schoolmaster sniffs: 'Just think how many runs Bradman would have made had he held the bat correctly.'

From an Australian perspective, it all seems a uniquely English muddle, everyone just being first a little too polite, then rather too panicky. It is Pietersen's unpredictability that makes him such a formidable opponent; for the England and Wales Cricket Board to be so unready for such an eventuality seems wilfully obtuse. What is it that administrators do again? That's right—they administer. In fact, it's all they have to do. What happens if they fail? Where players are dropped and coaches are sacked, administrators abide, one feels, saved from clear accountability only by lack of obvious authority.

Six months before an Ashes series is a rotten time for pronouncements; who knows what might happen three hours before an Edgbaston Test? But there is an eerie sense that history might be repeating itself. From time to time over the last twenty years, England has seen the light at the end of the tunnel in its Ashes travails; on each occasion but one, it has turned out to be Australia's disappearing tail-lights. Come July, the teams' manpower should be nicely balanced— in which case it will, even more than usual, be a question of whose minds are the more readily disintegratable.

19 JANUARY
MATTHEW HAYDEN

Farewell the Strong Man

The retirement of Matthew Hayden almost calls for one of EJ Thribb's mock heroic valedictions:

So
Farewell then
Matthew Hayden
'Mental disintegration'
That was your catchphrase
Keith's mum pointed out that you have a higher Test
    average than either Viv Richards or Denis Compton
But I found you as interesting as your nickname
Frankly
Haydos

The International Cricket Council found a form of farewell perfectly reflecting popular ambivalence, first announcing confidently that Hayden was 'in the top 10 Test batsmen and top 20 ODI batsmen of all-time' according to that unimpeachable acid test of batsmanship 'the Reliance Mobile ICC Player Rankings', then clarifying in response to protests that the rankings did 'not necessarily mean he is the 10th-best Test batsman or 18th-best ODI batsman in the history of the game'. Well, obviously.

Like Keith's mum, Ricky Ponting stuck to the tried-and-true benchmark of averages. 'Look through the history books of the game and try and see if there has ever been a better opening batsman,' he demanded, with a confidence that could only come from having not read any of those history books, with their references to such obscure old lags as Hobbs, Hutton, Gavaskar, Greenidge, Morris and Mitchell. Veterans of life under the Caribbean cosh, meanwhile, suggested some qualitative difference between ducking Roberts, Holding, Garner, Croft, Marshall, Ambrose and Patterson and sauntering down the wicket to Andy Blignaut and Trevor Gripper.

All of which is vaguely unfair. Sportsmen don't have the discretion to choose their eras. There were other challenges for Hayden too. In an age of incessant international competition he had to be fit, and was so constantly until the last year. In an era of sporting ego he kept his effortlessly hale, while shrewdly manipulating those of others.

Few *mano a mano* duels in cricket in the last decade have rivalled the one involving Hayden and Shoaib Akhtar in Sharjah in October 2002. Hayden scored 119 in more than seven hours, winding Shoaib up until the fast bowler was roused to fury—fury that, because of the 50-degree heat, quickly depleted him. Six months later, in the World Cup final, Hayden stared down a wild-eyed Zaheer Khan, belting a flurry of boundaries then baiting him with equally sweet timing. 'Smell that, Z?' he smirked. 'That's your house in India burning down.'

Nonetheless, Hayden's rude average and talismanic

presence obscure some instructive wrinkles in his record. He was, for example, considerably more effective in Tests at home (average 58) than away (average 41), benefiting from trends in Australian groundsmanship to playalike pitches everywhere, hard as granite and flat as linoleum.

Few players with such an extensive career, furthermore, can have scored such a great proportion of their runs under a single captain. In the four years of Steve Waugh's leadership, Hayden averaged 67; in the rest of his career, 41. This seems more than coincidence—Waugh's all-out aggression emancipated his burly colleague, as other more circumspect approaches did not. Under Mark Taylor, with whom Waugh the captain is often unflatteringly compared, Hayden averaged just 24. Was this linked to Taylor's own travails as a batsman for part of that time, to Hayden's drafting in place of the popular and successful Michael Slater, to a general sense of time borrowed?

More than most players, I suspect, Hayden benefited from continuity, not just of his own selection but of others. During his peak of proficiency, he paired up with Justin Langer; they became as familiar and inseparable as a pirate and his parrot. It's a factor in matters of team composition that selectors would do well to heed: a player is not just a sum of his abilities, but also his relationships with comrades. And no cricketer is so dependent on another as an opening batsman on his partner.

In his recent book *Seeing the Sunrise*, which quotes almost everyone bar EJ Thribb, Langer put Hayden's form lapse a few years ago down to his 'allowing the future to distract him': 'He was saying how busy his calendar was for the next year and how he was worried about fitting everything in ... Matty Hayden, like all true champions, learned his lesson and came out better and stronger than ever.'

Maybe; maybe not. In the middle of his recent run of outs, Hayden was talking optimistically about jetting off to play for the Chennai Super Kings in the Champions League, and the further-off goal of that fourth Ashes tour of his. The comeback was always being deferred—at last, indefinitely.

Rating Hayden exactly is more difficult than either the Reliance Mobile ICC Player Rankings or the history books make it appear. Hayden was very much a cricketer of his time: a time of big bats and shrinking boundaries favouring his strength-through-joy methods; of sharply improving rewards that made it worth his while to keep playing to the age of thirty-seven; of nonstop competition not only maximising his opportunities to perform, but also taking the edge off opponents who might have subdued him.

For professionalisation and globalisation have not bestowed their benefits equally. Where a Matthew Hayden can undertake the drill of hitting a thousand balls in the nets before a Test innings, it is physically impossible for Brett Lee to bowl a thousand deliveries. Batting is an easier art in which to groove oneself; bowlers are more susceptible to the vagaries of the day, fluctuations of confidence, ration of luck. Thus may Hayden have punched above his true Test weight, while Lee has perhaps never quite sustained the lofty heights and searing velocities expected of him a decade ago.

By the same token, I remember a remark of Michael Holding's many years ago, that he preferred bowling to Greg Chappell than Ian: Greg had the silken skills, he explained, but Ian had the power 'to embarrass you'. Hayden had similar capacities. A great many international bowlers will breathe more easily at word of Hayden's retirement—a tribute reserved for few.

Hayden's successor will be a New South Welshman named Phil—either 29-year-old Jaques or 20-year-old Hughes. Jaques is advantaged by the fact that Australia's selectors no longer seem to pick players as young as twenty, Hughes by the possibility that in a period of flux they just might.

Time was when successions in Australian teams were as smooth as the hand-offs of an Olympic relay team. There is a feeling just now that there may be a greater zeal for experimentation among selectors, and that queues might just be jumpable. It is a time in Australia ripe for the making of reputations: the twenty-four hours following the Twenty20 debut of 22-year-old David Warner were only slightly less euphoric than VE Day. Nobody gives the team a chance in South Africa. Opportunities are made of this.

11 MARCH
AUSTRALIA IN SOUTH AFRICA

The Shock of the New

Brief, protracted, V-shaped, W-shaped, amphibious landing craft-shaped: no consensus exists about the form, depth or duration of the recession that may or may not be about to lurch into depression. The same seems true of the credit-worthiness of the Australian cricket team, who were below investment grade at the end of 2008, but two months later are AAA-rated thanks to a stimulus package of new caps.

While England's batsmen padded their averages in Bridg-etown, Australia's battled to protect theirs in Johannesburg. Conditions worked in Australia's favour: rather than pick a specialist slow bowler for the sake of it, they chose a batsman, Marcus North, who made a priceless hundred, then turned out not to need the spin option anyway. But they deserved their fortune. Like Mark Taylor at Old Trafford in 1997, Ricky Ponting sacrificed a short-term advantage to obtain a long-term objective in batting first, and saw it pay off.

In Durban, the toast was young Phil Hughes, whose twin centuries contained 166 in boundaries while other batsmen struggled to come to terms with the conditions. There was a great deal of learned talk about the influence of the tide; for Hughes, it was the tide that comes in the affairs of men. Much of the bowling burden, meanwhile, was borne by the chalk-and-cheese Victorians Peter Siddle and Andrew McDonald, who last season were stalwarts of the Sheffield Shield not obviously destined for higher honours.

It was hard to believe that this was the same Australian team so lacklustre in Melbourne, and for good reason—it wasn't. At the time of the Boxing Day Test, Australia's selectors were holding steadfastly to the form-is-temporary-class-is-permanent line, particularly in the case of Queenslanders Andrew Symonds and Matthew Hayden. But Symonds looked smaller-than-life, nursing a damaged knee and a distracted mind, while Hayden had grown like Hillary Clinton towards the end of the Democratic primaries, hanging around to no purpose yet unable to believe it was over. The turnaround has been a testament to the capacity of new cricketers to restore fortunes, and perhaps a retort to the conventional wisdom that the team that stays together plays together.

It has been Australia that, over the last decade or so, has most publicly promoted continuity of selection as a cardinal virtue, depicting it as a key to success—albeit that this sometimes smacked of a confusion of cause and effect. Over the last couple of years, though, other countries have succeeded through more venturesome selection: Sri Lanka with Ajantha Mendis, Bangladesh with Shakib Al Hasan, even England with Graeme Swann. The unexpected star of the southern summer was JP Duminy, already a substantial figure, while New Zealand's best were also new arrivals: Daniel Flynn in the Test matches, Grant Elliott in the Chappell–Hadlee Trophy.

A Test debut is not what it was. 'I'm really proud of the kids,' said Australia's coach Tim Nielsen during the Test at the Wanderers, but he must have been talking about his own. Marcus North came to the crease with a decade of first-class cricket, almost 9000 runs and experience at five counties behind him. This might be the first major share-market crash of Phil Hughes's lifetime, but he has already played national representative cricket in India, Pakistan and Malaysia.

Big cricket, moreover, offers experience fast: fifteen months after earning his first cap, Mitchell Johnson collected his twentieth at Kingsmead. It also depreciates its assets quickly, particularly those involved in bowling fast: witness the cruelled careers, after early success, of Stuart Clark, Shaun Tait and Ryan Sidebottom, among others.

With this in mind, there is much to be said for promoting players before the bloom is off the rose—before long-term injuries take their toll, before the novelty of all those frequent flyer points wears off, before fat Indian Premier League offers instil a preference for cricket in twenty-over instalments. Selection is often said to involve a judgement of whether a player is 'ready for Test cricket'. Perhaps it should also include an assessment of whether Test cricket is ready for a particular player. The batsman whose technique has not been extensively scrutinised and the bowler whose fitness has not been compromised by years of hard labour might well enjoy advantages outweighing their 'inexperience'. The opposite is also true. Making a comeback in economic policy-making circles, Keynes might also have something to teach cricket selectors, once describing the very human preference for tolerating conventional failure over taking a chance on unconventional success—a premonition, perhaps, of the Test career of Ian Bell.

For fans, too, the refreshment of new talent to enjoy, savour, dissect and debate is a tonic not to be underestimated. Economic data of the last week has Australians sensing suddenly that things will get worse before getting better. That the same might not be true of their cricket team might make that a little easier to bear.

10 APRIL
THE 2009 AUSTRALIANS

New Kids on the Blockhole

Four years ago, Ricky Ponting came to England with an Australian team of the talents, rich in runs, wickets and experience—and, of course, however briefly, turned the Ashes over. Whatever befalls the touring party retracing those steps, the scenario will not be the same. Ponting's men have their best cricket in front of them; they do not have great futures behind them.

Mitchell Johnson, Peter Siddle, Phil Hughes, Nathan Hauritz ... their names lack the ring of McGrath, Lee, Hayden, Warne. But there can be no complaint about the nature of their initiation, for they have survived turnover in Australian ranks not seen in decades. If Australia's cricket empire is passing before our eyes, it is not for want of experimentation. Those who board the Emirates airliner on 27 May will be the survivors of a pretty rigorous attrition.

Johnson's career has been led in dog years. Eighteen months ago he was still awaiting his baggy green; today he is closing fast on 200 international wickets, while his 694 Test runs include a maiden hundred. It will not be his first time in England, for he was here ten years ago as an under-19. But between times he almost forsook the game, demoralised by stress fractures in his back that cost him his state contract in 2003. He is a different cricketer. It was his speed that first excited onlookers; now it is his swing, especially the in-ducker he showed off in South Africa, for a few overs at least. Johnson lacks only a genuine presence. He goes about his work with an almost innocent air, a smile seldom far from his lips, like a shy boy in the kitchen at a party. But his career has quickly become substantial, his value enhanced by fast-improving batting. With little backlift, flourish or ostentation, he has hit almost as many sixes in twenty-one Tests (fifteen) as Michael Clarke in forty-seven (sixteen).

The bustling, broad-shouldered Siddle has attitude to burn—the sort of attitude, and willingness to work, that endears a cricketer to his captain. Thrown into a Test in Mohali last October, he bowled more overs than anyone else in a team being beaten out of sight on a pitch tailored for Sachin Tendulkar. His nickname Vicious is derived from a shortening of his surname to Sid, although he might have earned it with his Merv-like bounce and growl. Siddle has been stymied during his seven Tests, but never subdued, and is exhibiting a happy knack of breaking partnerships against the run of play and defeating well-set batsmen. Nor is shyness his problem; indeed, he impresses as the kind of companionable soul who at a party might coax his mate Mitch out of the kitchen.

For some of the last fifteen years and most of the last ten, the sight of Matthew Hayden taking guard, carving up the ground beneath him as though for trench warfare rather than cricket, has been a proclamation of Australian intent. However, as the exercise last summer became about Hayden digging a deeper and deeper hole for himself, the selectors had a host of replacement candidates: Phil Jaques, returning from injury after back-to-back centuries in his third and fourth Tests; Indian Premier League prodigy Shaun Marsh; perennial nearly man Brad Hodge. Then, through the pack, burst fully formed Phillip Hughes, just turned twenty but making very adult quantities of runs for New South Wales, and peaking at the precise moment a decision was needed.

Everything about Australia's youngest new Test cap in a quarter of a century has shown a similar knack of timing. If he lacks Hayden's Tarzan-like stature, the lithe left-hander already scores almost as quickly, and South Africa's short, fast efforts to intimidate him at Kingsmead failed hopelessly. He has a country boy's self-containment and a professional's fastidiousness, his determination to master English conditions evinced by his decision to sample county cricket with Middlesex before the Tests.

The figure whose gap has been hardest to fill, for Australian cricket as well as the tabloid papers, is Shane Warne's: it's been like trying to cast a sequel to *Hamlet* with Bernardo as the chief protagonist. Since Warne's exit, the slow-bowling mantle has been shared around the country, with Stuart MacGill and Beau Casson from New South Wales, Cameron White and Bryce McGain from Victoria and Jason Krejza from Tasmania all trying it on for size, and Andrew Symonds from Queensland and Marcus North from Western Australia filling stop-gap roles. At the end of the process, the man in possession was fresh-faced finger spinner Nathan Hauritz, toiling twelve overs to obtain each wicket, but giving away only 2.7 runs an over. Australia might yet elect to go without a specialist spinner in certain scenarios, using North's *faute de mieux* right arm slows in addition to his fluent left-handed strokes. But Hauritz may be lucky to have emerged just as Warne's shadow receded; Stuart MacGill must wish he could be starting his career right now.

There is a faint historical echo to this Australian team. In 1972, selector Neil Harvey told skipper Ian Chappell that he might not have the greatest squad to lead, but it was a 'team of goers'. So it proved: Greg Chappell, Dennis Lillee and Rod Marsh, little heralded, helped Australia split the series, building the basis of a powerful dynasty. Australia's selectors will fancy themselves at a similar historical hinge point now. The faces are so different, meanwhile, that a re-run of 2005 is now the remotest of possibilities—and that, of course, from Australia's point of view, is a very good thing.

27 MAY
RICKY PONTING

Come Again?

Ricky Ponting was born in December 1974, just as England's last few fingers were being prised from the Ashes. He came to cricket maturity during an era in which the trophy was regarded as an Australian birthright, and never looked a more accomplished leader than in the summer of 2006–07 when England was flayed five-zip. But this northern sojourn could be regarded as his Ashes acid test.

While nearly 23 000 international runs appear to brook no argument, Ponting's Test average in England is a modest 42, as distinct from 58 everywhere else. Ponting prospers when the ball is bouncing, for his pet pull shot, and deviating relatively little, so he can play his bread-and-butter leg-side strokes with impunity; English conditions sometimes make it hard for him. He compiled a century in his first innings on English soil, but his two hundreds since came amid first a defeat, then a draw interspersing two defeats. Snip the relevant Tests out and his average dwindles to 28.

Ponting bounced back smartly from the disappointments of 2005; indeed, some part of him probably found them motivating, for he tackled the rematch with a cold, iron will. Yet he returns to England with a team that looks to him now more than ever. Australia's middle order in the last year has been as volatile as the Dow, with Michael Hussey tentative,

Andrew Symonds vagrant and Adam Gilchrist absent; even vice-captain Michael Clarke, with whom Ponting shared the Allan Border Medal, was below par in South Africa. Sometimes, as during Ponting's asymmetric double of 101 and 99 during the Boxing Day Test, he seems to be playing in a different game to his teammates. Once in a while, especially during the gruelling Nagpur Test in which his captaincy was harshly belittled, he might almost have wanted to.

In Ponting's favour this summer is England's attack, which will hold few terrors for him. That bodes well for Australia. Twenty-seven of Ponting's thirty-seven Test hundreds have been compiled in eighty-nine winning causes—a remarkable ratio. He has the gift, in other words, not merely of making runs, but of making them in circumstances that combine successfully with the efforts of others—his runs have what an economist would call a multiplier effect. The effect seems to work on himself too. Ponting always looks the more poised and decisive captain when he is batting fluently, with the corollary that, unlike Mark Taylor, his leadership authority appears to dwindle, or at least not be exercised so confidently, when his scores thin.

Although the team Ponting brings with him is nominally less impressive than four years ago, it looks more assuredly his. There is no John Buchanan speaking in riddles. There's neither Warne nor McGrath, neither Hayden nor Langer; the batting's other survivor is flinty Simon Katich, to whom Ponting is close. The attack bowled for Ponting in their dreams before the chance to do so in reality, and have played under no other captain. Ponting's trip matters in another ineradicable respect. While he has taken steps to be fresh for his Ashes challenge, skipping both the Indian Premier League and Australia's Dubai derby against Pakistan, it's possible that this will be his last trip to England, for he will be in his thirty-ninth year by the time the next is scheduled, and his young family is expanding.

Towards the end of his career, Steve Waugh was apt to invoke India as his 'final frontier'. England now occupies a similar place in Ponting's objectives.

2 JUNE
ENGLAND

Carpe Diem

For most of us, 'standing up' is an act of courtesy on buses and trains for the pregnant and the elderly, and in effect a kind of standing down or aside. In the world of sport, 'standing up' is something that marks progress in stature and maturity, a seizing of the day, or of the moment.

In English cricket, it is 'standing up' on Ashes days that still count the most, and in 2005 it was Kevin Pietersen and the Andrews Flintoff and Strauss who collared those opportunities best. 2009 will offer a host of 'standing up' chances to England's next generation: how they seize them could determine the trophy's custody.

Australians have already had a glimmer of that generation, most particularly when they played Essex at

Chelmsford in 2005 on the eve of the Oval Test, desperate for good cheer to take into that must-win game. On the first day they struck, and were struck by, two recent England under-19s: Alastair Cook and Ravi Bopara. Cook made a double hundred and Bopara a hundred, peppering a short square boundary, preparing the way for exciting careers that duly came to pass.

Cook, now twenty-four, has been marked out for high honours since boyhood, when at Bedford School he had a succession of top-class coaches: Andy Pick, Richard Bates and Derek Randall. Although he could move his right foot and bend his right leg more, he has all the strokes when he chooses to play them. He has guts, too: his 116 in Perth made in Ethiopic heat against a rampant attack, was England's best innings of the last Ashes series. Glenn McGrath arrived at the press conference that evening as Cook was leaving, and stopped to pump his hand. 'Well batted mate,' said McGrath genuinely. 'Great knock.' It was a generous, even paternal gesture, like a headmaster congratulating a diligent pupil.

If Cook has a fault, it's that he still looks a schoolboy—young, slim, a little diffident, a stranger to struggle. He might detain a bowler a while, but is unlikely to hurt him: he didn't manage a Test six until he top-edged a pull shot in Wellington last year. His conversion rate, moreover, is likely to remain poor if he continues to be a one-pace batsman, incapable of accelerating after reaching fifty. He should take a leaf from the book of Stephen Fleming, another good-looking left-hander, who recalibrated his game after the first half of his career was disappointingly short of hundreds.

Bopara, by contrast, has all the confidence Cook appears to lack, and more. The best thing about Bopara is his three summer hundreds against the West Indies; the next best is his three winter ducks. Some young England players have never quite recovered from similar setbacks, but having squandered one opportunity, Bopara made the most of the next. He has seized the number three berth in England's order with a technique and a temperament that look more suited to number five, although number threes are scarce everywhere: it is hard to think of who will succeed Ricky Ponting for Australia when he retires. As admirable a quality is self-belief, one wonders if Bopara has the humility to learn. Australians are apt to cut down players, like Daryll Cullinan and Keith Arthurton, who are a little ahead of themselves. England's coach, his former Essex teammate Andy Flower, will need to keep Bopara's feet on the ground.

James Anderson has had all sorts of reasons to get ahead of himself, exciting everyone who saw him as a teenager and quickly becoming a marketable commodity in the over-heating, overhyping English sports environment. He was first spied seven years ago, taking 9 for 57 at Blackpool, by Marcus Trescothick, who promptly urged his coach Duncan Fletcher: 'You've got to take him to the ICC Champions Trophy and keep him in mind for the one-dayers in Australia and the World Cup after that. He's only nineteen, but I'm telling you he is that good.'

So four years after becoming a first XI at Burnley Cricket Club, Anderson found himself opening England's attack during the VB Series of January 2003, before oozing promise during the World Cup. Young, handsome and fast, he had the world at his feet when injury and form checked his headway, and he came no closer to adorning the 2005 Ashes than acting as twelfth man at The Oval, somehow missing out on a British Empire Medal in the process. Rebuilding has been worth it: nobody in England swings the ball as much and at such pace, and he had as many reasons to recall the recent series against the West Indies as the majority of players had to forget it. Anderson's problem is that when the ball does not swing, he bowls a trajectory and hits the bat at a pace that favours fast scoring. While he has worked hard at his game since, there were times in Australia during 2006–07 when he looked as predictable as a bowling machine.

Nobody held the door ajar for off-spinner Graeme Swann while he was away sorting his career out. On his first England tour at twenty-one, he spent too much time in Phil Tufnell's company—good for the broadening of one's life experiences, but not an unmitigated good for one's cricket. Returning to county cricket, he seemed to lose his way, like rather too many players of his type, slipping behind his teammate Monty Panesar in the Northants pecking order, and rediscovering his mojo only after moving to nearby Notts, who won the County Championship in his first season. Worming his way back into national calculations last year, he made his debut against India in Chennai, then overhauled Panesar in the Caribbean.

Swann is an aggressive off-spinner who flings himself into his delivery with an idiosyncratic double whirl, and attacks the stumps: his thirty-four Test wickets have contained five bowleds and sixteen lbws, and include twelve left-handers. His natural gregariousness equips him well for dealing with the media, whom he handles as adeptly as anyone in his team. Like all slow bowlers, he needs love and encouragement, and assistant coach Mushtaq Ahmed seems to have provided it. The test will come when his so far brief and successful Test career hits a speed bump. The attrition rate among finger spinners in this big-batted, small-grounded era of international cricket is high and rising.

England's selectors handle their young players better than they did in the 1980s and 1990s, having then been prone to expecting immediate results; as Lord Home once said in the context of a young colleague's critics, they were like impatient gardeners, gauging a tree's progress by digging it up to examine its roots. They might now be accused of the opposite characteristic, of operating too much of a closed shop, even if it is surely preferable to their earlier methods. But then, there is the similarity between the two kinds of 'standing up': for how long is it expedient to wait before someone does it?

4 JUNE
ANDREW STRAUSS

Best of Breed

Where captaincy is concerned, the English tradition is that one chooses the best captain and the Australian tradition is that one chooses the best player. In his first six months as

England's first-choice skipper, Andrew Strauss has come close to satisfying both prerequisites, as perhaps befits a player of English parentage educated in Australia, having been born in South Africa.

Strauss might have kept the job he first held almost three years ago in Michael Vaughan's stead, but the claims of Andrew Flintoff were preferred, and his own form tapered in an unhappy and unsuccessful team. He has looked this time more ready, and a more complete player, the steady pair of hands that English cricket needed after the tensions and turmoils of the Kevin Pietersen/Peter Moores axis. Apparently he gets nervous, but you'd never know it: he walks down the pitch between overs like a man fetching his post from the mailbox. Nor does he waste energy on unfulfilled starts: on seventeen of the thirty-one occasions he has passed 50, Strauss has transited to 100.

Perhaps his most useful characteristic coming into such a summer is that he knows Aussies well. As a 20-year-old Middlesex batsman he got into the habit of changing next to Justin Langer: nobody else would go near Langer, such was the intensity of his temper after getting out. The seriousness rubbed off, and the competitiveness was hardened by a season playing alongside the young Brett Lee at Mosman soon after. Two years later, Strauss was captaining his county; two years after that, he was making an accomplished hundred on Test debut at Lord's, and reaching 1000 Test runs within eight months.

The Ashes defeat at Lord's in 2005 as part of a fancied England team set Strauss to brooding, amid which he bumped into another former Middlesex teammate, New Zealander Stephen Fleming. 'You don't know how close you are,' Fleming told him. 'The Aussies are definitely ruffled by your quicker bowlers ... If you guys keep playing the way you are, you're a real chance.' So it proved. Unlike some English cricketers, then, born into an era of Australian dominance, Strauss has never been in awe of his opponents.

All the same, it was his struggles against Australia in 2006–07 that led to the only significant setback in an otherwise gilded career. Misadventures with the pull shot, misfortunes with the umpires, misalliances in the touring party: all gradually unhinged Strauss's game, and led to nine months' penance. He missed Duncan Fletcher, his old England coach, and his comeback was tentative until a last-chance 177 against New Zealand in Napier last year.

Since then, he has looked a batsman of growing substance and authority—sometimes slow to assert himself but hard to absolutely contain; still strong square of the wicket and off the pads, but with improved timing down the ground and enhanced discretion in playing cross-batted shots. He now leans on the front foot when he essays the pull, in order to keep the ball down. He is as yet a circumspect captain, although he has had much to be circumspect about after coming into the position in January 2009 with neither a full-fledged coach nor a real mandate. With Andy Flower, like Fletcher a Zimbabwean, he has since formed a productive relationship. This Ashes challenge comes early in their joint mission, but they will establish something of their own heritage if it succeeds.

6 JUNE
ANDREW SYMONDS

Excess Baggage

Andrew Symonds has an alcohol problem. So does Cricket Australia. Andrew Symonds has been forced to make public acknowledgement of his problem, and is to pay a massive price by returning home early from the ICC World Twenty20. Cricket Australia is still in denial.

Time was when Symonds thought seriously about giving cricket away in favour of rugby league. He evidently made the wrong call. Had he defected to the Brisbane Broncos as he fantasised of doing, sneaking out of a team hotel to have a few beers while watching the State of Origin, as he is meant to have done in London, would then have been a compulsory rite of passage, not the subject of mandatory punishment; indeed, had there not been a gang bang involved, he probably would have been regarded as an underachiever. Whatever the case, there do seem two extraordinarily different codes of behaviour involved. League has made the blind eye as much a feature of the game as the grapple tackle, while cricket appears to have imbibed Mencken's famous definition of puritanism as 'the haunting fear that someone somewhere is enjoying themselves'.

There's a third standard involved too. Twenty years ago David Boon, now a Test selector, staggered off an airliner at Heathrow the worse for a record number of beers consumed en route from Australia—a record that he has parlayed into a healthy post-retirement career, and which has for years been celebrated by one of Cricket Australia's major sponsors. Cricket Australia, then, has more than a nodding acquaintance with the irresponsible drinking for which it has convicted Symonds.

In hindsight, it appears obvious that Symonds should never have been picked: his behaviour smacks of a player who wasn't quite sure how much he wanted to be in England in the first place, who wasn't comfortable about his role in the team after being excluded from the Ashes squad, who had come from the big money and VIP treatment of the IPL, missed his old mucka Matthew Hayden and found accounting for his whereabouts every moment of the day to be inhibiting, maybe even a little demeaning. If you're trying to resist the enticements of alcohol, it's such pressure situations where willpower is most routinely found wanting.

While Symonds is easily confused, furthermore, here he has some right to be so. For the last year he has been undergoing a 'rehabilitation' process described in the woolliest terms of therapeutic ideology—the creepy, infantilising tyranny of the twelve-step program. Now, having been pardoned and excused for more significant misdemeanours, he finds himself in a zero-tolerance environment and punished for a trifle. Why? Because, Ricky Ponting explains, impressionable young teammates might have their heads turned. But if that's the case, then what does that say of Ponting, who after leading Australia in fifty-six Tests and 184 one-day internationals is still so unsure of his own authority? Was the environment really so risky, so fraught? Perhaps Symonds has more faith in the common sense of his comrades than his captain.

The counterargument is that Symonds has been penalised not for falling off the wagon, but for deviating from the straight and narrow path set him by Cricket Australia and the team 'leadership group'—that peculiar oxymoron. But how realistic were those expectations, and how proportionate is the penalty? And while personally I think James Sutherland is a better man than this, some will also see CA's as an opportunistic punishment, meted out because Symonds has so forfeited public popularity that he can easily be made an example of.

Whatever the case, Symonds would be justified in reflecting on the example set by his newly punitive employer. Many people in this country drink to excess rather too often. This is sometimes because they are helpless to do otherwise, but also because advertising, by associating itself with the positive reputation of sport, has successfully reinforced the idea that alcohol is integral to any good time in the making.

CA certainly loves a drop. CUB is doubly represented in the board's sponsorship portfolio: its number one beer brand, VB, with its now rather tired vaunting of Boony, Beefy and Warnie, is a Platinum Partner; its number one wine brand, Wolf Blass, is a Gold Partner. Diageo is also a Gold Partner in the brand name of Johnnie Walker; Asahi Breweries is an Official Supplier as the owner of Schweppes. Andrew Symonds' sin lies partly in his demonstrating why the makers of alcoholic beverages so love their sport, the hankering to watch State of Origin and the itch for a beer having in his mind acquired reflex connection.

In the mid-1980s, an earlier cricket maverick in Greg Matthews was penalised for publicly disavowing tobacco, thereby offending Australian cricket's then sponsor Benson & Hedges. One wonders how CUB will feel about the message from CA that drinking while watching sport can actually destroy your career.

1 JULY
AUSTRALIA

The Team that Plays Together

For the last year, arriving at a view of the strength of the Australian cricket team has been like fathoming the true seriousness of the global financial crisis. Was this recession or depression? Was one observing shoots of promise or the bouncing of various dead cats? Even now, it's tempting to extrapolate from single events: a scarcity of runs here, an excess of no-balls there, the observable reality that the best Australian bowler of the World Twenty20 was Dirk Nannes. But this is a long tour—by far the longest of all tours these days, and it is sustained effort and consistency that will count.

The journey will be shadowed everywhere by recollections of 2005, with a concomitant search for omens and auspices. Already, however, it presents the clearest possible contrast. Four years ago, Ricky Ponting brought a team of galacticos, eight of its members touring for the third time, Shane Warne for the fourth. Played on an Xbox, the series would have been an Australian whitewash. If Brett Lee fails to make the cut at Cardiff next week, by comparison, the members of Australia's attack will not have a Test in this country between them, while only the captain can boast a Test century on English soil.

In one respect, this Australian team is almost bound to acquit itself better than its predecessor: it will be more harmonious. For as the core of Australian champions has disbanded over the last four years, it has emerged just how discontented and disunited was their XI's 2005 incarnation.

In his uncommonly candid autobiography *True Colours*, Adam Gilchrist has described how adversity quickly plunged the Australians into recriminations, particularly against their coach John Buchanan:

> Everyone seemed agitated and anxious, and not responding to each other. No one was responding to any of the efforts Buck was putting in. In fact, there was coffee table talk from guys becoming frustrated and disillusioned with him, saying he wasn't providing the service they wanted from a coach ... They were saying his ideas had grown stale. He loved meetings, and guys were grumbling, 'Why do we need more meetings?'

Buchanan, meanwhile, has offered a mea non culpa in his manual cum memoir *If Better is Possible*, explaining how he left most of the quotidian coaching duties to his assistant Jamie Siddons 'so I could spend more time being strategic about our preparation ... finding tasks and experiences to expand the horizons of the players'. With strategy to burn, but no tactics to speak of, Australia barely won a session after Lord's. No wonder there was muffled laughter in Australian circles a few weeks ago when it was revealed that Buchanan had accepted the ECB shilling this summer.

Gilchrist also describes how 'personality clashes had disrupted relations between the wives and partners', reporting: 'A guy would go to dinner with his partner and hear bad things about someone else's partner; you could be sure that the same was happening somewhere else in reverse.' Coaching chaos; WAG wars: no wonder they were calling cricket the New Football four years ago. This time it will be different, and not simply because Buchanan's successor Tim Nielsen has more invested in lateral movement than lateral thinking.

In the antipodean summer at home, Australia twice surrendered winning positions to a South African team that played them on their abilities rather than their reputations. There were scattergun selections and peculiar perseverances, especially involving Matthew Hayden, whose failures accumulated like unshriven sins, and Andrew Symonds, who kept gazing at his bat as though willing it to turn into a fishing rod. It was a rude awakening.

Yet once the team was on the road in the return series, the esprit de corps was palpable. On flat pitches, South Africa would almost certainly have prevailed again. But unexpectedly spicy surfaces emboldened Mitchell Johnson, Peter Siddle and Ben Hilfenhaus, and some none-too-brainy bowling then let fresh-faced Phillip Hughes loose. There were valuable chippings-in from new caps Marcus North and Andrew McDonald. And their captain suddenly had a new lease on life, speaking of an 'exciting time in my career' and the 'opportunity for this bunch of guys to forge their own identity'.

For while a tour can be isolating and repetitive, it can also focus minds and encourage mutual reliance. Young Australians are noted for being eager travellers, and this team looked like a bunch of students in a gap year bent on savouring everything their journey had to offer. It was as impressive a bounceback as Australia's legendary World Cup campaign ten years ago.

To refresh my memory of Ashes past before leaving Australia, I re-read the cycle of tour diaries that Steve Waugh commenced in 1993. Inevitably they recall Edna St Vincent Millay's line about life: not so much one damn thing after another as the same damn thing over and over. Yet they also show Australian teams of his era intent not only on winning but on enjoying one another's company. There are lots of running gags, silly pranks, communal activities, cheerful rivalries, plus a bemusement among the Australians that their English counterparts demonstrate no such predisposition. By 2005, as Gilchrist would lament, the roles had been reversed.

'We didn't have to look far … to see an example of a team cohering as a team: we were playing against them.'

So while most of what is written about this Ashes series will concern specific contests and particular skills—Hughes's strokes versus Anderson's swing, Pietersen's power versus Johnson's pace—don't underestimate the aspects to which no outside observer is genuinely privy: intangibles like togetherness, morale, individual ambition and collective pride. If the times are more austere, the Australians already have experience of organising their own bailouts.

6 JULY
2005 v 2009

BC/AD

Tired of forecasts? Me too. The Ashes phoney war of 2009 hasn't been quite as protracted as four years ago, when it perforce spread the length of two one-day series, but it already seems long enough, and it has done little more than repeat an obvious truth: here are two workmanlike cricket teams without much to separate them.

Some other obvious truths warrant elucidation too. For one thing, don't expect a repeat of 2005, that unforgettable mixture of drama, thriller and panto, with England playing Jack to Australia's giant on a five-Test beanstalk. Warne, McGrath, Gilchrist, Ponting: their failing to keep the Ashes proved even more compelling than their obtaining them, because it ran so much against the long-established grain. This Australian team lacks the pre-existing personalities for such a fairytale.

There can be no repeat of the sense four years ago of nationwide involvement in this Ashes series either, of anyone and everyone watching the sphincter-tightening final morning of the Edgbaston Test. Today, into the fourth year of BSkyB's control of broadcast rights, in a country where the venue of the First Test holds just 16 000, cricket seems actually to have narrowed the niche it occupies in British life.

Yet let's not be too downbeat. Even five years ago it seemed too much to hope for the Ashes ever being more than a periodic recertification of Australian superiority. Five weeks ago it was almost possible to forget that Test cricket existed, so successfully was Twenty20 hogging the limelight. And the forecasts, the endless cogitation over what 'might' be important, what 'could' be a factor, are not only a kind of tribute to Test cricket's myriad varieties and potentialities, but to the idea that it is susceptible to the interrogation of a thoughtful mind, and over the course of a series will genuinely demonstrate which is the better cricket side, rather than merely the better cricket side on the day.

The weather seems full of hope too. It pelted in Cardiff this morning, but the skies this afternoon are full of blue, and the outlook for the five scheduled days is favourable— something not to be taken for granted in South Wales. That forecast may prove more important than anything we journalists have written.

7 JULY
ASHES PAST AND PRESENT

A New Angle

The series begining tomorrow in Cardiff between Australia and England will be the twentieth I have watched as fan and journalist, enough to make anyone feel their seniority, if not their obsolescence. I have vivid recollections of each, and senses of change to go with the general continuity, two of which have stood out recently in contemplating my very earliest memories of Ashes competition.

In 1974–75, the first Ashes series I saw, Derek Underwood provided the only variation on right-arm over-the-wicket, and John Edrich and David Lloyd the only alternatives to the phalanx of right-handed specialist batsmen (Wally Edwards was there for Australia too, but, I hope he'll pardon me saying, never for long).

Cricket today is almost unthinkably different. For the third consecutive Ashes series, the opening batsmen on both sides will be left-handed; likewise four of Australia's top six. Mitchell Johnson is the first left-arm quick to lead an Australian attack in England since Alan Davidson. Simon Katich should purvey his chinamen. England have excluded Ryan Sidebottom, but look like opting for Monty Panesar.

This not only makes for more various cricket, full of angles and inclines, tugging techniques in different directions, but adds a particular layer of complication to a captain's deliberations in England, where the gradient of grounds is a factor as in no other country, and pitches are soft enough to wear unpredictably. How, for instance, might the excavations of Johnson's front foot enhance Graeme Swann's effectiveness to Ricky Ponting and Michael Clarke, Australia's best players of slow bowling? How might they complicate the challenges to Matt Prior's glovework?

In 1974–75, Australia enjoyed an advantage in sheer pace not experienced by an Ashes side for twenty years: Jeff Thomson and Dennis Lillee omnipotent reigned, and Bob Willis could be testingly quick at times too. Yet we never knew exactly how quick they really were. Pace was judged the old-fashioned way, correlating the length of the ball with the height of the bounce, the batsmen's degree of hurry, and in due course their observable flinching. Australians were happy enough with two ideas: Thomson and Lillee were very quick, and they were on our side.

With the modern craving for quantification has come the tyranny of the speed gun, these days rather more reliable than the one I saw at Headingley eight years ago that clocked (an admittedly languid) Alan Mullally at 11 miles per hour. With Brett Lee's incapacitation for the First Test, reported the *Daily Mail* this morning, England achieved a vital edge in speed:

> The Aussies are still not short of pace and Mitchell Johnson can deliver at 94mph—although Stuart Broad is capable of matching that. England also have

Freddie Flintoff, Jimmy Anderson (both 93mph) and Graham Onions (90mph), and there is always Steve Harmison (96mph) in reserve. Peter Siddle (92mph), Shane Watson (90mph), Ben Hilfenhaus (89mph) and Stuart Clark (88mph) are Ricky Ponting's other pace aces.

Never mind the scoreboard—look at the speedo!

Silly stuff, of course, and not merely because it looks like Shane Watson will only clock 90 miles per hour this season in a sports car. Cricket's infatuation with precision of pace also contains a degree of looking backwards: the game remains stubbornly imperial in a metric age. Yet it has had its impact, even at first-class level. 'In the county game whenever the TV cameras turn up, so does the speed gun,' admits Martin Bicknell in his recent autobiography. 'All the bowlers are conscious of it; they want to be the fastest bowler on show.' He says that what worried him most about his return to Test cricket was how surveillance would confirm the passage of years. It seems almost like spoiling the game to recall that the most effective seam bowler in the corresponding Test four years ago was the slowest on either side: Glenn McGrath.

One element of the Ashes that has not changed is the acute sense of accompanying expectation, this one not least of all, the anticipation sharpened by the summer's structure, Twenty20's unrelenting roll. Everything stops for the Ashes; everything *has* to stop for the Ashes. Let's hope it is worth the stopping, and always will be.

7 JULY
ASHES 2009

Battle Renewed

First versus fifth in a nine-team competition does not usually pack spectators in. Test cricket tomorrow provides an exception: an extraordinary expectation surrounds the resumption of its originating rivalry, the Ashes. It is the first five-day international match played at Cardiff's picturesque Sophia Gardens, where flags fly bearing such improbable greetings as 'Wales says G'Dai' and 'Old South Wales Welcomes New South Wales'. Otherwise, the feelings occasioned are purely atavistic.

Not only do 132 years of history bear down on the competitors, but in form terms there is barely a chink of daylight between them. Save for the eighteen months following 2005's Oval Test, Australia have held the Ashes twenty years. Yet Ricky Ponting's team hold their Test match blue riband chiefly by virtue of past rather than present strength, having lost two of their last four series.

England, meanwhile, have been undergoing the latest stage of a long-term rebuilding that commenced at around the time of the Suez crisis. Back in harness after injury, nonetheless, are the talismanic presences of four years ago: Kevin Pietersen and Andrew Flintoff, and a captain in Andrew Strauss who looks the part more completely every day.

That said, form seldom seems a reliable indicator around

Ashes series. Just before the opening Test of the 1997 series, Nasser Hussain found himself in a deep trough and told his old county mentor Keith Fletcher: 'God, Fletch. What am I going to do? I've got the Australians this summer and I'm in the worst form of my life.' Fletcher reassured him: 'You'll be right, old mate. You're thinking about it too much. Next week's a Test match. Completely different.'

So it proved—Hussain made a match-winning double hundred—and the 'complete difference' of Ashes series has perhaps never been more pronounced than since the rise of Twenty20 cricket. The five-Test series was for a century the standard unit of international cricket rivalry. Now it is only played by the format's pioneers over the course of Ashes. Late last year, England played the West Indies in a Twenty20 match that lasted less than three hours for a grubstake of US$20 million. For England to now spend seven weeks playing Australia mainly for honour and glory seems almost unpardonably decadent.

In a contest so close, availabilities will be crucial, so the cruelling of Brett Lee's Ashes series with a low-grade abdominal tear is an acute setback to the Australians, for whom he had gone from being eleventh-hour inclusion to form bowler in one spell of reverse swing against the England Lions last week. Alas, in turning the clock back to his salad days, he demonstrated the toll of time on his physique, and side strains are notoriously stubborn injuries, even for a bowler of Lee's noted recuperative powers.

On a pitch forecast to be soft, and to take slow turn on the last two days, Lee might not have been decisive. But his absence makes likelier the selection of Nathan Hauritz, whose misfortune it is to be an Aussie slow bowler in the post-Warne years; if Hauritz does not play here, it is hard to think of circumstances under which he might be picked. There were no indications of preference yesterday from Ponting, who looked like he was preparing to take Shane Warne on at poker.

What does seem clear is that the teams favour different formations. Australia's plan seems to be to bat deep, as they did successfully in South Africa, and a team with Marcus North, Brad Haddin and Mitchell Johnson at numbers six, seven and eight will be no pushover. England are preparing to include a fifth bowler, the attacking option, and recent history suggests that the attacking team wins.

In 2005, with the invariable exception of Warne, the Australians played beige cricket, trusting in familiar routine to neutralise England's disarming flair. The situation recalled Churchill's description of the war cabinet during the Dardanelles campaign: 'We conferred endlessly and futilely, and arrived at the place from which we started. Then we did what we knew we had to do in the first place and we failed as we knew we would.'

In 2006–07, Australia won the first toss, took the first innings, and hardly relinquished the advantage thereafter, grinding England underfoot in five consecutive Tests. Ponting was so determined to discomfit his opponents that he warned teammates against overfamiliarity: Flintoff, popularly 'Freddie', was to be called 'Andrew'; Pietersen was 'Kevin' but never 'KP'.

If it is too much to hope for a repeat of the glories of four years ago, a summer of attacking intent will be a welcome affirmation of the Ashes' pre-eminence. The rivalry is prestigious, ancient, savoured among its traditional public. But this series will begin in a stadium that holds a fifth the number of people who turned out yesterday to watch Cristiano Ronaldo stroll along a catwalk in his Real Madrid strip. Rich as its laurels are, Ashes cricket cannot afford to rest on them.

Part II

FIRST TEST

Sophia Gardens, Cardiff
8–12 July 2009
Match drawn

8 JULY

Day 1

England 1st innings 336–7 (JM Anderson 2*, SCJ Broad 4*, 90 overs)

It wasn't 2005—and how often will that be said this summer?—but the first day of the Ashes of 2009 provided just the sort of tense, fluctuating, attritional cricket widely foreseen, with one exception of lavish, almost stupendous stupidity.

For a player of his quality, Kevin Pietersen finds some decidedly odd ways to get out, like an ace contract bridge player who keeps forgetting the rules to 500. Today it was a premeditated fetch to leg from 3 feet wide of off stump that looped to short leg via his helmet, ending three hours of diligent application, and England's top score.

The beneficiary of Pietersen's largesse was a deserving one: Nathan Hauritz, said so often not to be Shane Warne that he must sometimes feel like issuing a pre-emptive public apology. Hauritz would have been an onlooker had Brett Lee maintained fitness, and still seems to lack the variation necessary to prosper at the top level. But the delivery in question could hardly have been improved on, drifting away towards slip and dragging Pietersen so wide that he almost ended up on the neighbouring pitch.

It was a day from which Australia and England could take a good deal, even if neither team was quite good enough to retain the initiative for long. The Australian pace bowlers who did Ricky Ponting proud in South Africa again competed tigerishly, gaining from the air the movement that the pitch did not offer. Each of England's top six stayed a while, and Strauss won an advantage with the toss, Australia's fate of batting last shaping as a significant challenge.

The rest of Strauss's day was less satisfactory, Australia's bowlers reminding him of his misadventures with the pull shot down under in 2006–07. Strauss looked determined to abjure the stroke—under-edging one, genuflecting to another, picking a third off his hip—but neither played nor left the last ball of the twentieth over, which carried on from glove to slip. It was a wicket for thought, Johnson having thought just enough, Strauss perhaps a little too much.

There was a pleasing vernacular quality to the pace attack: plumber's mate (Johnson), bricklayer (Hilfenhaus) and woodchopper (Siddle) all put in suitably tradesman-like performances, and all were picked ahead of the banker (Clark), doubtless to Alistair Darling's satisfaction. Ravi Bopara's Ashes debut, by contrast, did not resolve the doubts aired about him by Shane Warne a couple of weeks ago—specifically, that he cared too much about his appearance. There are certainly some ostentatious flourishes to Bopara's game—the curtsey as he lets the ball go, the frozen front

elbow after every defensive stroke—and there were opportunities to evaluate them as the only scoring stroke of his first
twenty balls was an inside edge to fine leg. One of Pietersen's
skittish singles caught Bopara unawares, perhaps admiring
his image on the big screen. He prospered only when Siddle
allowed him width, and was ultimately hoodwinked by
Johnson: five overs after miscuing one slower ball safely, he
did the same terminally.

On such a pitch four years ago, Warne would have
bowled in the first hour, having probably pestered Ponting
for the new ball. Hauritz had to wait until 2 p.m. before
coming on with the Taff and tour figures of 2 for 260 behind
him. At first he did basically what one expected of him—little
wrong but nothing special, improving Australia's over rate
but providing little grist for his Cricket Australia tour blog.

Pester power seemed in evidence in mid-afternoon when
Michael Clarke was deployed for five rather pointless overs
in harness with Hauritz, a period in which 37 runs accumulated at no apparent risk to either Pietersen or his escort Paul
Collingwood. Clarke is known to fancy his bowling, to the
extent of it being a team in-joke, but Hauritz surely needed
more pressure from the opposite end. Hilfenhaus, meanwhile,
went almost thirty overs without bowling, and when he did
return had Collingwood caught behind and Pietersen trapped
plumb in front of all three, except that Billy Doctrove agreed
with perhaps only Pietersen's parents and gave him not out.

The reaction was as much a study as the delivery. Hilfenhaus groaned, Ponting chuntered at length, but the appeal
was in truth a little ragged, some fielders interested also in

the caught behind. Umpires are sensitive to ambiguity, and influenced by uniformity of appeals, so it wasn't only Shane Warne's bowling that was missed today but also his undiluted, unreconstructed come-on-ump-you-know-they're-here-to-watch-me-bowl cries for justice. Over the years Australians have been criticised with some force for the pressure they place on umpires; it would be perverse to criticise them for the opposite, but it is a habit they may have lost to their cost.

The Australians did not have long to rue their luck, for Clarke soon after shelled Pietersen at cover—in much the same fashion that Pietersen shelled Clarke at a critical juncture in the corresponding Test four years ago, leading to Clarke's best score in England. Hauritz's coup to remove Pietersen soon after, however, ruined yet another 2005 parallel.

By now, in fact, the 2005 parallels were beginning to fade in significance—the day was taking on a pleasing quality of its own. The last session featured 142 runs in thirty-one overs, including an hour's crisp and fluent strokeplay from Matt Prior and Andrew Flintoff, and four wickets, including two in fourteen deliveries with the second new ball to Siddle, who provided an object lesson in sticking to the basics and trying nothing too fancy—a lesson Pietersen is still to learn. A few more sessions like this last, in fact, and this series might begin standing on its own feet rather than seeming at times a pretext for interspersing highlights of four years ago.

9 JULY

Day 2

Australia 1st innings 249–1 (SM Katich 104*, RT Ponting 100*, 71 overs)

Ricky Ponting and Simon Katich today made England's bowlers look bad and England's batsmen look even worse. On the first day, each of England's top six got in, looked around, had a dash, and squandered their chances of a big score. There were no heroics in Australia's reply, but constant application and mutuality in a 189-run partnership from 337 deliveries that culminated in centuries for both—centuries that showed no sign of abating at stumps.

This was old-fashioned Test match batting, the stand containing only 60 runs in boundaries but 53 singles, the swapping of left- and right-hander forcing bowlers into constant changes of line. Australia still trailed on first innings by 186 at stumps, although there will be nine overs to settle in tomorrow with this rather soft and ragged old ball before England are eligible for the replacement they clearly hanker for.

Ponting has been quietly out of sorts this last year, with only a single century in his previous twenty-one Test innings— not a truly obtrusive form lapse, but a definite tailing off in such a hundred glutton. He has looked overeager to assert himself early. There was no haste or hurry today, however, and hard as it was at day's end to remember a dashing stroke, it was almost impossible to recall a false one.

For Katich, this was the continuation of what now amounts to a purple patch: his sixth hundred in his last sixteen Tests, a period in which Australian runs have been scarcer than in earlier years of plenty. John Howard's face in the crowd today recalled the former prime minister's comment, before one of many political comebacks, that the times would suit him, thinking of the drift to conservatism in periods of economic anxiety. The cricket times have suited Katich, with his perseverance and plain virtues.

England began the day expansively, its tailenders making hay against an attack looking a tad weary from earlier exertions. Graeme Swann made batting look as easy as anyone, stating afterwards that England's plan was to wrest the 'momentum' of the game. Except perhaps in the giant slalom, is there any more overestimated sporting fancy than 'momentum'? If anything, England bowled before lunch as if they had too much.

Having carefully prepared not to bowl short and wide to Phil Hughes, Anderson and Broad bowled ... short and wide, denying themselves the opportunity to swing the ball without denying Hughes the opportunity to play his pet square slash. The intent was doubtless to rough Hughes up a little, after his over-reported overthrow by Steve Harmison in the tour game at Worcester, but England's openers were far less precise, and their trajectory did not present the same challenges.

The taller, stronger Flintoff's first over to Hughes almost justified his selection on its own, five deliveries from round the wicket bouncing sternum-high, a sixth veering past the outside edge, bowler following through down the pitch with his jolly jack tar's swagger. The ball hit Prior's gloves with a satisfying whack rather than the clang that sometimes emanates from them. Hughes was in Year 10 when Flintoff made the Ashes of 2005 his own: this must have been like living out a still-fresh schoolboy fantasy.

Hughes's technique is such that he makes Katich, no apostle of the MCC coaching manual, look like the acme of orthodoxy. Offering the bowler a lingering look at middle and off, he is capable of cutting deliveries more conventional batsmen would leave, and his timing is peachy sweet; apparently defensive pushes rushed boundarywards today, belying the slow outfield. But his footwork is a complicated minuet that, with Flintoff clocking 93 miles per hour, soon began to look hurried; the eventual under-edge did not ultimately surprise. Both this match's batting prodigies have now found hidden complications in a hitherto straightforward game, Ravi Bopara having battled inconclusively on the first day.

Thereafter, it was all care and plenty of responsibility. In his pomp, Ponting would never have allowed a finger spinner to bowl a spell of 7-5-7-0 as he did Graeme Swann after lunch today, but he was a man intent, overhauling 11 000 Test runs like a Murdoch racking up millions—enjoying the sensation, but never losing sight of the purpose.

The pitch was slow and Australia not exactly allegro either, each 50 taking slightly longer: 81, 85, 89 and 93 balls. But apart from an alarm when Katich was 56, when a less assiduous umpire than Billy Doctrove might have judged him lbw to Swann, and a false start or two when Ponting was 99, the game became one-way traffic.

In the Australian dressing room during the last half-hour, a padded-up but disarmingly animated Peter Siddle could be observed preparing to mount the nightwatch, chatting away to his comrades as though he couldn't wait to be out there. He had to settle for knowing that his two late wickets on the first day now look to have been a vital contribution; at the present rate he might not enjoy his turn with the bat until Sunday afternoon.

England have spent years trying to invest their cap with the authority of continuity and uniformity that Australia derive from their baggy green, to some effect. But what, in the meantime, have they done to their jumper, whose resemblance to the kind of rubbishy promotional windcheater one finds in the bottom of a sponsor's showbag is shown up by the old-fashioned elegance of the Australian cableknit sweater (albeit that this, too, is now marred by Cricket Australia's cock-eyed, lopsided logo)? Just theorising here, but might this change of attire have something to do with either money or the latest theory about the performance-enhancing properties of rubbishy promotional windcheaters?

The old jumper should not perish unmourned. On its standard 1981/2005 highlights default setting, Sky has today been showing footage from Headingley twenty-eight years ago, and Ian Botham is impossible to imagine in anything other than the traditional English long-sleeve, tight on his torso, bare of embellishment. How someone could feel a sentimental attachment to the successor item entirely eludes me. As for the shirt, don't get me started.

10 JULY

Day 3

Australia 1st innings 479–5 (MJ North 54*, BJ Haddin 4*, 139 overs)

There was a thoroughly organised, integrated and cohesive team effort in the field after tea in the First Test at Sophia Gardens today. Unfortunately for England, it involved the deployment of the covers. Fortunately for England, it was in response to rain that has cast Saturday's play into doubt, shortening the time available for Australia to prosecute an impressive and growing advantage.

Australia accreted 230 runs in the sixty-eight overs played, notwithstanding a two-hour weather interruption and an interlude of ten and a half overs containing three wickets for 32. One of those wickets was Simon Katich, tripping over a full pitch from Anderson for 122; another was captain Ricky Ponting, dragging Panesar on for 150; the third was the out-of-sorts Michael Hussey, after the false promise of a big innings at Worcester, and having been struck a glancing blow on his helmet by Flintoff. In the context of this innings, it constituted a veritable avalanche.

All told, there has been about an hour of committed, aggressive, genuinely dangerous English bowling in this match. Unfortunately they have been in the field for five and a half sessions, and between times have looked desperately pedestrian. Where Hilfenhaus in particular obtained consistent swing and Siddle impressive bounce, England has laboured in search of both. The sharp turn Hauritz achieved on Thursday morning must have been due to the curvature of the earth, because Graeme Swann and Monty Panesar have been patiently picked off without disturbance—Swann too full, Panesar too short.

England can point to an almost blameless catching record, the one chance to go down being a difficult return to Flintoff when Katich was 10. All that can be inferred from this, however, is the general sense of Australian control pervading play since an hour after lunch yesterday, prolonged today by Michael Clarke and Marcus North in a partnership of 143 runs from forty-two overs; the latter was still in possession at stumps on 54.

Clarke, made to fumble round his front pad four years ago like a man groping for a keyhole in the dark, seemed to be seeing the ball especially early today, for he had time to spare, choosing his strokes with precision and discrimination. Where even Ponting and Katich had been content to play the slower bowlers from the crease, Clarke came down the track with youthful relish, confident he would come to no harm. A fine straight six off Panesar was almost as good as a lip-smacking pull shot for four off Flintoff.

Australia's vice-captain has been a strangely anonymous figure on this tour for someone with a fiancée and a financial profile such as his. The structure of the trip has had something to do with this. Like his captain, Clarke has no love for Twenty20, at which he averages a modest 17 and strikes at a positively lethargic 106 per 100 balls. His 83 from 145 balls today, however, seemed like a breath of Clarke at his bonny best, now a little further back than commonly imagined. To the end of last year's series in the Caribbean, Clarke's Test runs had been accumulated at 56 per 100 balls; since then, under the pressure of increasing adversity, his scoring rate has dropped to 47. It does not seem much, but it is a reflection of the harder times for Australia over the past year, and Clarke's growing sense of responsibility for counteracting them.

Today we saw again the cocky, smiley Clarke, pleased with a form of cricket he is at home with, and the freedom of 3 for 325 when he came in. When he pulled the boundary that confirmed Australia's lead, one half expected him to take a little jump and click his heels like Danny Kaye. He has made a good start on putting to rights a curious disparity between his record in Australia, where he averages 58, and in other climes, where he averages 40. England may yet test a technique seemingly susceptible to the moving ball—although first they will have to move it.

North cut some capers against Panesar when sweeping out of the rough, but otherwise looked exactly as one would expect a batsman who has experience with five counties behind him: utterly at home and awake to everything. He made 219 here five years ago for Durham when there were probably fewer people in the crowd than there are in the media centre this week. A tall, thick-set figure, he looks like the obstacle he is threatening to become in this series.

Another obstacle to both teams has been standing at the Cathedral End these three days, there being considerable grounds for griping about the burden of proof required for an lbw by umpire Billy Doctrove, inscrutable to the degree that one almost wishes to place a glass slide over his mouth. His name makes it sound like he could inspire his own sect, the Doctrovians, dedicated to clamping down on all expressions of bowling pleasure—a sort of umpiring branch of the Plymouth Brethren.

In his defence, Doctrove gave way sufficiently to adjudge Clarke caught at the wicket—a good decision, from the merest of gloves, during the twenty-five-minute resumption after the rain. But he resumed his killjoy ways by proceeding to offer the batsmen the light despite the agency of floodlights, in use for the first time in a Test match in the United Kingdom.

As the players adjourned for the last time, a group below the media centre rendered perhaps the drunkest chorus of 'Bread of Heaven' ever attempted, making up for in gusto what it lacked in accuracy. England's attack should be made of such stuff.

10 JULY
RICKY PONTING

True Believer

One of the numbers in the Barmy Army's Ashes songbook teases Ricky Ponting that England contains antiques older than his country. The oldest player on either side in this series will probably appreciate a reference to comparative youth. The name 'Ricky' still savours of boy prodigy or teen idol, but Ponting has surveyed his dressing room these last few years with the aura of the venerable.

The members of that dressing room have returned Ponting's gaze with something approaching awe. Like the later Allan Border, he has become captain to a circle of cricketers who grew up watching him play. They look to him for the kind of craftsman's runs he has provided at Cardiff, and for the robust link he represents to past success.

Cricket can be unforgiving. Ponting perished yesterday to the first error he made, a slight misjudgement of Panesar's length. That he had 150 on the board will have been a consolation to Ponting, although not as much as it would be to other batsmen. He is an avowed perfectionist, almost a puritan of batting—one of the reasons he has never warmed to Twenty20, which he argues masks technical deficiencies as it privileges big hitting.

At the indoor nets where I often train in Melbourne,

the walls are dotted with the usual posters spruiking bats, bits and bobs, and one newspaper photo that the owner has had laminated: Ponting cover driving—big stride, perfect balance, low to the ground, bat at the end of the follow-through, elbow still high. 'Because *that's* how to do it,' the owner explained when I asked why.

So it is. There have been better batting exhibitions than Ponting's in the last two days, but it is hard to imagine a better batting tutorial, both in terms of stroke production and organisation. There were even some strokes not normally associated with Ponting: off Flintoff, a soundless leg glance for four and a genuine hook for six.

England successfully resisted the temptation to bowl too straight at him, instead nagging away outside off stump, but Ponting was up to that, puncturing the covers with five boundaries. He tormented Swann particularly, picking 31 effortless runs from the 36 balls he received, while Katich sweated over 30 from 94 off the same bowler.

About the batting, of course, we knew. By his consistency as a Test batsman—passing fifty better than once every three innings—Ponting has made the splendid commonplace. About the captaincy, more doubts are harboured, although they might be out of date.

Ponting's leadership still attracts plenty of criticism in Australia, particularly from ex-players who remember their era as one of nonstop flair and innovation. For sure, there remains some truth to the assertion that he does not deviate far from basics. But captaincy is in the main not a public event: it is the leadership in a dressing room, in a hotel, on a team bus, at training. And in this respect Ponting is, from all accounts, far better than he was.

Ponting is no arm-around-the-shoulder captain with a degree in people, the famous Bachelor of Brearleyism. In his early years he could be terse, gruff, not from lack of feeling, but because the expression of it did not come naturally. Jason Gillespie tells a story about being omitted from the Trent Bridge Test four years ago. Ponting accosted him at training and said simply: 'Has [chairman of selectors] Trevor [Hohns] spoken to you yet?' When Gillespie indicated Hohns had, Ponting grunted 'OK' and walked away.

Flash forward to last week when, just before the Cardiff Test, Hussey, Clarke and Ponting addressed their team in turn about the significance of the Ashes to them. The earnest Hussey delivered a poem, the polished Clarke did a video presentation. Ponting spoke simply and frankly, reminiscing about the feats of the Waughs and the bluster of Merv, but making it clear that he was every bit as proud and more of what the team had accomplished recently in South Africa. Some of this was doubtless the sportsman's preference for the recent over 'ancient history', but it was also a reflection of how he has been rejuvenated by the vim and vitality of his young side.

If Ponting did not set Statsguru on fire in South Africa, he has perhaps never looked a more authoritative captain, because the authority was yielded as well as commanded, there being no Warne, Gilchrist or Hayden to, however unwittingly, dilute it. Not since Border in his Horatius years has an Australian captain described an XI more truly as 'my team'.

Ponting has been made over off the field also by a new manager, media buyer James Henderson, whom he met through the foundation that emerged from a visit to the oncology ward of the Sydney Children's Hospital five years ago, and which endows causes associated with research into and treatment of childhood cancer.

The day Ponting was appointed Australian captain, he was costumed as an aerosol can of deodorant for one of his many endorsements. Since signing up with Henderson, he has projected an image more in keeping with the office occupied by Bradman and Benaud, and less like that of a sandwich board for hire. Through a website, Run Ricky Run, fans can even sponsor Ponting per run this summer for charity: with a little creative accountancy, Stuart Broad's half-volleys could prove to be tax-deductible.

Ponting inevitably will have been said to have 'made a statement' by his 150 here, as though this is itself a statement rather than a particularly insipid cliche. For Ponting has always made statements this way—what matters is that he now makes statements by other means.

11 JULY

Day 4

England 2nd innings 20–2 (AJ Strauss 6*, KP Pietersen 3*, 7 overs)

There's positive thinking, there's wishful thinking, and then there's cloud cuckoo land. Asked at the press conferences after the third day about the prospects for this First Test at Sophia Gardens, England's James Anderson announced insouciantly that his comrades were 'not thinking about a draw'; no, their aspirations were only of victory.

Even then, it was difficult to work out how Anderson saw this occurring, short of the Australians being incapacitated en masse by swine flu, or Freddie Flintoff developing a revolutionary reverse swing harnessing the power of carbon credits. And nothing observed today suggested other than that Anderson the night before had been talking through his expensively sponsored hat.

It was bad enough that, when rain ended proceedings almost on the stroke of tea, England was 219 runs in arrears with eight wickets remaining to negotiate the last day. What had preceded it was a catchweight contest all too reminiscent of the grim 1990s, Marcus North and Brad Haddin almost sauntering to hundreds, as Australia's innings assumed the epic proportions of the country's fourth-highest Ashes score, with an unprecedented four centurions. Their partnership was not perhaps so priceless as the 113 they added to turn the tide of the Johannesburg Test in February, but it was even more effectively sadistic.

With his huge reach, the 6 foot, 1 inch North presents a particular challenge to spinners; his sweep, a little rusty yesterday, became as unerring as a mechanical reaper. Not routinely strong forward of point, he also powered Broad through the covers early in the morning—as good a stroke as has been played this Test, and what West Indians call a 'Not a Man Move' shot. His luck was in too. He went into the nineties trying to leave Flintoff and guiding the ball inadvertently to the third man boundary; he could probably have batted right-handed for a dare and succeeded.

Haddin, who almost overhauled North despite his partner's 54-run head start, was more inclined to find room in the air, sweeping Swann majestically for six, then repeating the dose from Panesar with a pitching-wedge drive down the ground. He celebrated his hundred, and the 1000th Test run of his late-blooming career, with a consecutive four and a six to mid-on, hit so precisely, with minimal backlift and abbreviated follow-through, that they might have been aimed at particular figures in the crowd—perhaps his parents, who are visiting from Canberra.

Andrew Strauss's struggle to prevent boundaries left vistas of untenanted space for the batsmen to explore and exploit, it becoming almost difficult after a while not to score a run. Yet the boundaries barely ceased, and conceding singles to a left-right batting combination didn't help much either, the bowlers having constantly to recalibrate—to try, anyway. For fewer than twenty overs of Australia's 181-over entrenchment, in fact, were England's bowlers not confronted by such contrasting combinations. It has not been enough to explain their errors of line on its own, but it has been another thing for bowlers who already have much to brood on to consider.

The rotation of the strike slowed England's over rate to a walk; England's negativity slowed it to a stagger. They propelled only forty-two overs in more than three and a half hours, even though twenty-two of these were from Panesar,

Swann and Collingwood. Panesar in particular bowled wretchedly, so mechanical that he might conceivably be replaced by Merlyn, England's semi-legendary spin bowling machine; with a bucket attached, the apparatus would be just as effective in the field. Swann looked as challenging as anyone for half an hour before lunch, bowling a little slower than the day before, and gaining far more purchase as a result. But when Strauss opted to take the new ball on its falling due, such pressure as Swann had been able to maintain was released.

North and Haddin's first hundred runs took 170 balls, the second 98, squeezed in just before a sweetly timed declaration. Ponting was now doing everything right, deploying Johnson and Hilfenhaus from the opposite ends to the first innings, with immediate effect. Umpire Billy Doctrove then revealed a new characteristic: he gives them in the second innings. Inscrutable throughout the first ten sessions, he now fired Bopara out lbw without a second thought, although Hilfenhaus's in-ducker would have cleared the stumps with airspace to spare. Cook, who places his front foot rigidly, like a dance student following the black instructional footprint on a rehearsal studio floor, had earlier provided a more legitimate casualty.

Them, however, is the breaks, and Australia deserved their good fortune. With fine weather forecast tomorrow, and ninety-eight overs to bowl, they can expect more: in such situations, the luck always seems to favour the hunter over the hunted. Australia has cornered the market in positive thoughts, and with good reason.

12 JULY

Day 5

England 2nd innings 252–9 (105 overs)

Try explaining this to an American. For much of this First Test at Sophia Gardens, England were a shambles, humiliatingly poor, virtually finishing fourth behind Australia, Wales and then some daylight. Yet thanks to their last pair, James Anderson and Monty Panesar, who warded Australia off for 69 deliveries this evening, they go to Lord's with the series still 0–0.

Cue all sorts of cod psychology. Is it as good as a win for England? Is it a form of defeat for Australia? Ricky Ponting admitted last night that the visitors' dressing room was 'quiet' at the close, with the qualifier that this would only last for an hour or two. Andrew Strauss spoke of feeling 'pride' but mainly 'relief', with the admission it had been 'horrible to watch'.

Both sides have certainly learned a lot; in England's case, this has been at best salutary, at worst embarrassing. The Australians—captain, players and press—were feeling hard done by at the end, sensing perfidious Albion behind late on-field sorties by England's physiotherapist and twelfth man, which smacked of time wasting.

What's for sure is that the series needed just such a result: drama 2009 style, rather than a warming over of 2005. For this was a day's play full of plots, subplots and intrigues, a fine advertisement for what, in the spirit of Twenty20, will probably soon be called Four-Hundred-and-Fifty450.

Before play, Cardiff was enough to make any Melburnian homesick. Rain was pouring one moment, sunshine gleaming the next, with the best cricket weather probably at 6 a.m. Play began beneath cloud cover but by noon the arena was flooded with light, surprisingly warm, and full of fans trying to make the most of a day that few could see going past tea.

Pietersen apparently exchanged words with the tourists during the morning's warm-ups, when a ball he struck interfered with an Australian routine. It was his last effective stroke. When he batted, he went as close as one can to playing a shot without actually playing one: it was like smoking without inhaling. Two overs earlier, he had allowed Hilfenhaus to hit his back pad while letting a ball go that came back slightly; this time, he held his bat high as a ball zeroed in on middle. At the last split second, the bat began descending, but posthumously; the delivery held its line, collecting the top of off.

Pietersen might have been leaving on length, banking on the bounce to save him; Pietersen might have been leaving on principle, to show, after his first-innings indiscretion, exactly how responsible he can be. Who can say? The contents of Pietersen's head enthral English cricket fans, as the contents of Michael Jackson's spellbind the tabloids.

Whatever the case, his technique at the moment is a train wreck: balance amiss, front foot barely budging. This was a dismissal with a touch about it of Michael Vaughan, a high-class batsman who could nonetheless make a nonde-script delivery look like the proverbial sostenutor.

With Pietersen's dismissal, odds on an English victory were officially listed at 501 to 1. Longer than Headingley '81! Time for a plunge, surely! On the other hand, a pound's a pound. Five of them and you almost have enough for a cup of coffee in London. When Strauss was then caught at the wicket in Hauritz's first over, the odds shot out to 601 to 1. Here was a lost cause in which not even Dennis Lillee or Rod Marsh would have invested.

The Test would have been over by lunch had Katich been perched a couple of feet closer at bat-pad when Collingwood (11) got a glove on Hauritz. The next ball, too, rolled to within a micron of the stumps, until Collingwood's groping back foot interposed.

These alarms apart, Collingwood batted with commend-able coolness. No England player looks quite so grim on the field; none stretches his talents so far. Nor did he make the same mistake as at Adelaide Oval two and a half years ago, when the strokelessness of his defiance (22 not out in 198 minutes) cost runs that might have extended Australia's victory chase, although paralysis did seem to set in when England did not score a run in the first five and a half overs after lunch.

Awkward slip catches made to look simple accounted for Flintoff and Prior, and Broad completed a poor match lbw to Hauritz, having the nerve to shake his head afterwards when any umpire other than Billy Doctrove would have given him out first ball, hit on the boot by Johnson. The chirpy Swann provided Collingwood with the most productive support and also the most protracted, spinning the seventieth over out to ten minutes by twice calling for cold spray after he was hit on the arm and finger. He might have requested it a third time for his ears after some gratuitous advice from bowler Peter Siddle.

The second new ball finally did for Swann, lbw in what proved the mysteriously underbowled Hilfenhaus's twelfth and final over for the day. And at this pass, as the match came to its climax, Ponting seemed to miss a trick, depending on a swift Siddle but a wayward Johnson, then, anxious to squeeze in the maximum number of overs, Hauritz and North.

Siddle had Collingwood caught at backward point, and the Australians rejoiced again; Collingwood, devastated, could be seen in the dressing-room window for the rest of the innings, still wearing his pads. But Johnson bowled three wides in a sloppy six overs and, apart from some speculative running, Anderson and Panesar looked unexpectedly untroubled, the pace bowlers operating without a short leg, the spinners not extracting the turn they had on the second day. England went into the lead with 45 deliveries to go, an Anderson thick edge flying for four to third man, followed by another to point. The crowd was ecstatic. One half expected a chorus of 'Land of My Fathers'.

After North had bowled the 102nd over, England's substitute fielder Bilal Shafayat came on with fresh gloves, and their physio Steve McCaig with an urgent consignment of Juicy Fruit—or something. The message imparted was that the match was being played to time rather than overs, so it was essential to reach 6.40 p.m.—ten minutes before the scheduled finish, but the effective end because of the time required for a change of innings.

Ponting was decidedly unimpressed, and after another unscheduled visit he let the interlopers know it. Anderson, to his credit, was hardly more impressed. He turned away and looked faintly embarrassed: it could just as easily have worked Australia's way by disturbing the batsmen's concentration. Strauss later called it a 'misunderstanding', a convenient euphemism. But in the end, the 105th and last over beginning at 6.39 p.m., it probably did not entail any net loss of bowling time. Anderson met each ball from Hauritz with the deadest of bats, apart from the last, from which was run a final bye.

Actually, never mind an American. Try to explain this match, and the sheer fun and excitement of the final hour, with defensive shots being cheered to the echo, attacking strokes sending a chill up the collective spine, to Lalit Modi.

12 JULY
TEST CRICKET IN WALES

Sophia's Choice

Sophia Gardens in Cardiff, which last week became the 100th venue to host a Test match, is as picturesque as its euphonious name suggests: snug, tree-fringed, with the river Taff at one end and a pub called Y Mochyn Du (The Black Pig) at the other. Yet for all its old-fashioned airs, the ground may contain a glimpse of the future.

There was considerable controversy three years ago when the ECB recognised its second geographical jurisdiction by granting Glamorgan County Cricket Club the right to a Test, at the expense of traditional venues like Old Trafford and Trent Bridge. The Ashes of 2005 opened at Lord's in front of a crowd that loosened its collective egg-and-bacon tie to roar the home side on; the sequel has commenced in a stadium cradling a cosy 16 000 people.

The inaugural Test match in Wales owed much to the favour of the Welsh Assembly and the Wales Tourist Board, which stumped up £3 million for a top-to-bottom refurbishment of what had been a fairly rudimentary county arena. The clincher was then Glamorgan's guarantee of a £3.2 million profit—more than twice the best figure on offer elsewhere—and the rest is very recent history.

Disgruntled rival counties have since forced a revision of the Test match bidding process that expedited the Welsh bid. But the Welsh are very pleased with their Test, as well they might be, First Minister Rhodri Morgan describing it as a 'fantastic success' and prophesising: 'Whatever happens to the series and whatever the final result I think Wales was the winner.'

What about the rest of us? For all its aesthetic appeal, Cardiff still seems an incongruously low-key location for a Test match, least of all in Test cricket's one remaining marquee series since the suspension of competition between India and Pakistan. Its financial strength derives from a high proportion of corporate and hospitality seating, which takes up at least a quarter of the ground. Just after lunch on Thursday, when Andrew Flintoff was bowling a riveting, don't-look-away-now spell at 93 miles per hour to Phillip Hughes, the seats in front of the dining suites were deserted. The guests must have been dining on braised unicorn and ambrosia to prefer it to the feast of cricket in the middle.

The Barmy Army, the happy-go-lucky gang of supporters who rejoiced at England's every success four years ago and made them seem like a team of twelve, have barely been heard from: a chorus or two here, a bugle blast there. Rather than enhance the sense of drama, recourse to highlights of 2005 at any opportunity has tended to evince the relative serenity of proceedings.

What has happened in the intervening period? For one thing, English cricket is now broadcast on pay television, Rupert Murdoch's BSkyB, which almost four years ago made a knockout bid for rights that sent the BBC packing after sixty-one years. The argument was that the additional money would tend to the beneficiation of grass-roots cricket, and there is evidence that sizeable investments have been made. But the unquantifiable contraction of the audience has exacerbated a tendency to conceive of Test cricket as an exclusive game, for hardcore tragics only.

The other development has been Twenty20 cricket, which the English are apt to point out they invented, but which the IPL has since popularised and industrialised far more effectively. English cricket authorities have scrambled to keep up. Their plans for an England Premier League were foiled when their backer, Texan Allen Stanford, went the way of the South Sea Bubble; two quasi-domestic competitions are now mooted for next season.

The size of English grounds, none with a capacity greater than 30 000, has tended to preserve Test match attendance as a minority pursuit. In his recent autobiography, England's opening batsman Alastair Cook reveals that the only Test he had attended before his international debut in Nagpur was an Australia v Pakistan Match at the WACA while he was playing Perth grade cricket. With Twenty20 viewed as the more accessible and demotic version of the game, Cardiff suggests that Test cricket is to be repackaged permanently as a boutique entertainment, partly funded by £100 tickets and corporate dining suites, but subsidised chiefly by television. Which is fine as long as Test match broadcasting rights are bundled with those of Twenty20 and one-day internationals—but for how much longer will that be?

All of which makes a good story about English decadence and dilettantism, but it also has profound implications elsewhere, for it threatens to leave Australia as the last country in which Test matches, the oldest, longest and most satisfyingly complex form of cricket, are taken seriously as a mass amusement.

On 7 July, Sri Lanka and Pakistan finished one of the best Test matches of recent times, Pakistan losing eight for 46 to subside to a 50-run defeat. The final rites were watched by 2000 people. But the malaise in other countries is a familiar tale; we have always banked on the Ashes' continuing relevance and popularity. Australia remains Test cricket's number one nation. The question is not: for how much longer? It is: for how much longer will that matter?

13 JULY
FIRST TEST

Drawn and Quartered

After the Third Test of the 2005 Ashes was drawn in the gloaming at Old Trafford, Australia's last pair having survived the final four overs to save Ricky Ponting's blushes, England's captain Michael Vaughan drew his chagrined men together. Look at them, he said. Look at the Australians: their relief, their euphoria at merely saving a Test. That, he said, was a vulnerable team.

Now the roles are reversed, and it is Ponting who will be imparting the same truths to his Australians after England's last line of resistance, James Anderson and Monty Panesar, lasted the final 69 deliveries at Sophia Gardens. This was a rout: Australia lost six for 674 in 181 overs, England 19 for 687 in 212 overs. But Australia's inability to take a twentieth wicket leaves the teams all square for the Lord's Test beginning Thursday.

Australia went extremely close—an inch or two would have done it. England's main man on the last day, Paul Collingwood, should have been snaffled at bat-pad before lunch when he was 11, but Katich, a foot too deep, fell a fingertip short of the catch. The significance of the miss, as often in Test cricket, was understood only in retrospect, like one of those clues you kick yourself for overlooking in Agatha Christie: the telltale time of the delivery of a letter; a character's childhood fondness for E Nesbit. In hindsight, too, Marcus North and Brad Haddin should perhaps have trusted themselves to play through the bad light at the end of the third day; Andrew Strauss's remonstration with the umpires at the time is in retrospect deeply ironic.

The Australian press, as is their wont, have lashed the bungling English time wasting in the last few overs, and not without justification, although it was also, weirdly, part of the theatre of the climactic hour. Here is cricket, with its staggering variety of stipulations and prohibitions, and nobody was quite sure whether the day was being played to overs or time, while there was nothing to prevent physio Steve McCaig at the deathknock waddling onto the ground for no earthly reason. Had it been an IPL game, of course, one would have sensed at once the pretext for extra advertisements.

In hindsight, the Australians did not make the best of the time allowed them. That Ben Hilfenhaus bowled no more than twelve overs on the final day was puzzling to say the least. Ponting's faith in his 27-year-old off-spinner Nathan Hauritz was commendable, but spinners tire too, and Hauritz's fingers must have been worn out by his last few overs.

It's England, though, who have far more to chew on ahead of the rematch at a venue where they have won a solitary Ashes Test since 1896: cricket's curse of Tutankhamen. England's first innings of 435 covered a multitude of sins. Pietersen's technique has become disturbingly busy—the footwork too premeditated, the backlift too high—and he has lost the front-foot stride that made his height such an advantage four years ago. Constrained by his Achilles tendon injury, his movements resemble a frantic wobbling of a gear-stick that nonetheless leaves the car in neutral.

Much was heard in advance about the contrasting qualities of the members of England's pace attack. The skills differed all right; the mediocrity was unanimous. Flintoff was fast in his first foray, slower with each succeeding spell. Panesar was a selection of misplaced nostalgia: built-in obsolescence, success at the start followed by steadily diminishing returns, is common among finger spinners in international cricket these days, and he seems no exception.

The prediction for Lord's is another pudding pitch, as at Cardiff, implying that there will be few if any changes in either line-up, a case for the pace of Steve Harmison notwithstanding. Australia deserve to be favourites. Successful Ashes campaigns are built on a variety of emotional spurs: relief is not among them.

13 JULY
FIRST TEST

Australia's Overachievers

We should have known. A week or two before the First Test, the ICC announced that it was considering a proposal to reduce Test matches from five days to four. Such is the ICC's record of belatedly shutting stable gates after horse boltings and throwing pseudo-light on non-problems, a compelling vindication of the five-day format could not have been far away.

Thus the Cardiff Test, where time, apparently so abundant, became suddenly so scarce, one side hurrying, the other dallying, and where a day featuring a boundary only every five overs kept a full house fascinated down to the final delivery. As for all our percipient forecasts, they corroborated that aphorism of Niels Bohr: 'Prediction is very difficult. Especially about the future.'

The biggest underestimation was of Australia's attack, shorn of its star names McGrath and Warne, and then at the last moment of Lee. Critics before the Test agreed that Australia would struggle to take twenty English wickets. They were right—just—thanks to the rain, and to the survival instincts of England's last pair. Nonetheless, Hilfenhaus and Hauritz especially could be regarded as significant overachievers, accomplishing enough to be among the first chosen for the rest of the tour.

The Tasmanian Hilfenhaus ended up being clearly Australia's best bowler, operating at a fuller length than in South Africa and swinging the ball consistently. He also looks appropriately fierce, the kind of man who could shave before breakfast and have cultivated a moustache by lunchtime.

First included in an Australian Test squad in November 2007, Hilfenhaus's progress has been retarded by back injuries. Two years ago in Australia, a too-willing workhorse, he sent down 509 overs in a Sheffield Shield season—200 more than any other bowler. It has dogged him since and he has been treated more carefully, which may partly explain why Ponting looked elsewhere for his overs on the final day. The risks of overusing a bowler not quite ready have been revealed by England's Second Test selection today, with its doubts over Flintoff.

Hauritz's expression after dismissing Strauss, meanwhile, was of someone trying to look deadly earnest but incapable of keeping joy to himself. It was hard not to smile along with him. He came into the Cardiff Test almost as a token pick, pitted against two English slow bowlers on a pitch anticipated to suit them, and licked them both: by dint of bowling slower and more accurately, he eventually took 6 for 158 against their 1 for 266. No wicket was more crucial than Pietersen's on the first day—it will ramify for the whole series.

Pietersen is sometimes accused of thinking insufficiently about his batting; I suspect the contrary, that he's inclined to overmeditate and overcomplicate. Pietersen's discomfort with Hauritz in Cardiff arose not because the young Australian was posing insoluble dilemmas, but for the opposite reason:

here was a bowler he was expected to dominate. Hauritz had no ego to battle.

Thus Pietersen's insistence at stumps on the first day, to a roomful of sceptical journalists, that Hauritz was an opponent worthy of his mettle. England's star batsman has reached that delicate stage in a career where he is defending his reputation rather than merely making it. Hauritz is not a bad way to exploit it.

Australia's formula was so successful that it is hard to see why chairman of selectors Andrew Hilditch would alter it, except perhaps to include a fifth bowler, trusting Johnson to do the batting job at number seven, as surely one day he will. With the Second and Fourth Tests preceded by only three days' rest, the inclusion of a fresh bowler in each might not be inexpedient.

The desire for continuity, however, will almost certainly win out. And better can surely be expected of Johnson, who after sitting international cricket out between South Africa and the World Twenty20 might conceivably be underdone: his final six overs in Cardiff, with three official wides and several more moral wides, were the poorest Australian bowling of the Test, squandering the second new ball. He will have big shoes to fill on Thursday, his precursor Glenn McGrath having been the difference in the last three Ashes Tests at Lord's.

A five-day Ashes Test at Lord's: cricket does not come any more traditional. If what the ICC is entertaining comes to pass, it may be the last of its kind. Enjoy it while you can.

Part III

SECOND TEST

Lord's, London
16–20 July 2009
England won by 115 runs

15 JULY
ANDREW FLINTOFF

Going, Going ...

When he dismissed Phillip Hughes in Cardiff, Andrew Flintoff greeted the raised umpire's finger with a classic demonstration: shoulders back, chest out, arms aloft, muscles tensed—a proclamation of English purpose, like the prow of a man-o'-war. It was a pose familiar to anyone with remembrance of 2005, or who has been watching the endless re-runs of that series on Sky in the last two weeks.

It looked also like an attempt to rediscover the bygone magic that had made him the best all-round cricketer of his time, to rise above the increasing frailties of his anatomy that have ruled him out of twenty-five of England's last forty-eight Tests. It was in vain. Threatening at first, he was slower with each passing spell, picked off on a pitch that did his bang-it-in methods no favours. Twice he loomed with a bat, only to fall tamely. Seeing what looked very much like an end, he today embraced it, announcing at Lord's that this Test series would be his last, although he intends playing on in shorter forms of the game.

In truth, the continuation of his career has sometimes seemed a source of wonder. He is a big, heavy man who runs a long way and bowls a power of overs. The injuries he has forborne have seldom been breakdowns. Rather, they have been the result of long-term wear and tear: side strains, stress fractures, hernias, an ankle that needed four rebuildings. The last injury hurt most of all: a tear in the meniscus of the right knee sustained during Flintoff's third match in the IPL, where his total of 93 runs at 31 and two wickets at 54 cost the Chennai Super Kings US$1.5 million.

As expensive as this foray was for India Cements Ltd, proprietors of the Chennai Super Kings, it was more expensive for Flintoff. Keyhole surgery and an enforced lay-off were required. He began the Ashes of 2009 in form only at the bar, missing the bus on the team's 'bonding' trip to Flanders after a night of drinking for his country—an incident tactfully whitewashed by all concerned. The ECB turned a Nelsonian blind eye to their star all-rounder's behaviour, and, for all their seamy reputation, English red-tops are protective of their heroes.

Officially the knee injury was aggravated in the field at Sophia Gardens, but nobody really doubts that the swelling resulted from pounding in for thirty-five overs on an unsympathetic surface. So while it's an exaggeration to say that England squandered its Ashes chance at Kingsmead on 23 April, the attitudes of rival countries to the IPL are an instructive contrast. Where key Australians declined their invitations to the Trimalchio's dinner party of modern cricket, forgoing fat pay cheques in favour of being fresh when it mattered, both Flintoff and Kevin Pietersen took the cash, earning monies embarrassingly out of proportion with their performances.

Flintoff's Ashes record is a patchy one. He didn't make it onto the field in 2002–03, being invalided home with a hernia. He failed at Lord's four years ago, commenting ruefully after he had been bowled without scoring: 'I waited six years for that?' In 2006–07 he was a confused and confusing captain, undermining his coach Duncan Fletcher with constant drinking. Between times, for the last four Tests of that epoch-making 2005 series, he backed his ability and rode his luck like no Australian opponent in recent history, save perhaps Brian Lara and Sachin Tendulkar. Australian batsmen returned home regarding him the best fast bowler in the world. He was a gifted hitter rather than a Test-class batsman, as Ian Botham became, but his 102 four years ago at Trent Bridge showed a true Test-match temperament.

It's unknown still if Flintoff will play tomorrow. Officially he has passed his fitness test, but he will need careful handling if he is to survive the rest of the series as he intends. He walked across Lord's after training this morning, kit on back, bat in hand, stopped at the pitch under preparation to play a few shadow strokes at each end, and to survey the empty stands. Although the gesture at Cardiff was of the kind he will be remembered for, this sight at Lord's felt more in keeping with present realities.

16 JULY

Day 1

England 1st innings 364–6 (AJ Strauss 161*, SCJ Broad 7*, 90 overs)

Few days of cricket have been replayed so often and so senti-
mentally as the first at Lord's four years ago, with its violent
swings and wicked twists. Today will not demand the same
treatment in years to come, but its steadily shifting balance
of power was nearly as fascinating to watch.

England's captain Andrew Strauss ended the day with a
hundred against his name, an unbeaten 161 including twenty-
two boundaries; so did Australia's Mitchell Johnson, having
conceded 107, including nineteen boundaries. Johnson and
his comrades, nonetheless, might almost have ended up with
the better of the day, or at least a bigger share of it than
seemed possible at the halfway point, England's 0 for 196
having steadily dissolved into 6 for 333 despite Australia
being reduced in the afternoon to three specialist bowlers,
Nathan Hauritz having crooked a finger trying to catch a
red-hot return from Strauss.

Strauss's opening partnership with Alastair Cook spanned
190 minutes, 291 deliveries and some of the most ragged
outcricket Australia has perpetrated in the last year. Back-to-
back bowling in back-to-back Test matches is hard yakka for
quicks especially, and it showed. Johnson could simply not
get comfortable, although Ponting persisted with him until
his sling was slung; even at reduced pace, his star paceman

could find no control. Hilfenhaus began economically, and Siddle found the Pavilion End to his liking, going past Strauss's outside edge then endangering Cook's off stump with a couple coming back up the slope. But Cook won't go to a simpler fifty against Australia, and Strauss has faced more demands at Lord's in the nets.

In the field there were misfields, sloppy returns, a couple of dropped catches and overthrows—four from Ponting, throwing from mid-on, which the captain had then to watch several re-runs of on the big screen of the Tavern Stand, doing so with a chagrined smile. The worst offender was Haddin, who looked heavy-legged and hard-handed, standing up prematurely to the slow bowlers, slow to get moving to the quicks. He was fortunate that Hilfenhaus had overstepped when he shelled an outside edge from Strauss, then 48, but his glovework was poorer even than 15 byes suggested, the fumbling of one straightforward take from North causing him to pull away as though recoiling from an electric shock. His captain must have wished to administer one.

Strauss at his best is a batting minimalist: compact, into position early, playing the ball late, close to the body, under the eyes. Today he forced all the bowlers to bowl to him, sweating on errors of length, holding his bat from harm with the tiniest jink to one side. There were some high-class shots, including an on-drive off Hilfenhaus, and a precision square drive off North bisecting point and cover point, a stroke he repeated off Clarke. Otherwise, this was a century as laconic as one of his press conferences. Some Middlesex fans have tagged him Andrew Strauss OBE—Only Bats for

England. Four Test hundreds at Lord's, this one reached from the penultimate ball of the afternoon session, entitles him to some latitude.

Australia clawed their way back into the Test only after Johnson, quite against the run of play, trapped Cook within sight of a third Test hundred at Lord's. It was as simple as ceasing to bowl quite so many bad deliveries, forcing batsmen to go looking for scoring opportunities, which led them into indiscretion. Bopara played ambitiously around a straight one, and Collingwood holed out to mid-on in slovenly fashion off Clarke; had Hussey held onto Strauss's cut in the gully when England's captain was 105, Australia would have ended the day ahead.

Between times, Pietersen played an intriguing 42-ball cameo. He had the good fortune to take guard with Marcus North bowling, although he showed the part-time spinner greater respect than he showed Shane Warne here four years ago, and Ponting exerted pressure by inserting Katich under the lid at short leg and placing himself in the batsman's eyeline at silly point. To Hilfenhaus, Pietersen was again tentative, almost playing on, almost mishooking; he had no sooner played some strokes of authority off Siddle than he was adjudged to have nicked a leg-cutter.

The highlight of Johnson's day was obtaining some reverse swing in the last hour, which bowled Matt Prior through a gate that Siddle also opened in Cardiff. When Flintoff, in the opening date of his farewell tour, edged rather anticlimactically to slip, the day had turned topsy-turvy. It required Strauss to see his impressive vigil through to stumps for England to cling to the remnants of the morning's promise. His opposite number will feel he got off lightly, a day that could have gone pear-shaped bending back more like a banana.

16 JULY
MITCHELL JOHNSON

Blow-out

When he broke England's opening partnership today, Mitchell Johnson obtained his 100th Test wicket, having needed just a year and 250 days to achieve the milestone. Only one man, Kapil Dev, has done it more expeditiously.

Cricket teams have made a mardi gras out of celebrations for less, but it wasn't just the scoreline of 1 for 196 that made this look more like the result of a morale-boosting whiparound for flowers and a get-well card. It was also the protectiveness that a close-knit group extends to its most vulnerable member, the irony being that for the last year it has been batsmen who have needed protection from Johnson.

Johnson's lack of penetration on this tour has been only part of the problem. Worse has been his sheer lack of control, the waste of the first new ball here following the waste of the second in Cardiff, where it might have cost Australia a series lead—something which then was merely aggravating, but which now might prove vital. A low, round-arm sling looks dramatic when it works, a state of arrested development when it doesn't. The bat-and-bone-jarring speed and swing that Johnson achieved in South Africa a few months ago seem a distant memory.

Disappointed expectations arise also from Johnson's heritage. The English prefer their Aussie fast bowlers hairy and/or hearty, rather than fit to audition for a boy band, and the shy, polite Johnson smiles a little too often and too genuinely to radiate the approved histrionic hostility. Nor does he exude confidence. In the early stages of his career, teammates commented that Johnson was inclined to bowl faster in the nets than in matches, apparently reluctant to let himself go. Even at his quickest now, Johnson's simulations of menace, the regulation glares and glowerings, look like a fast bowling mime.

Above all, when Johnson is wayward, as he was today, his body language quickly becomes defensive. He talks to himself; he looks skywards; he pinches the bridge of his nose, like he's trying to keep something in; he feels *responsible*. The slope posed difficulties, perhaps also the Duke ball. There was no doubt to whom Brad Haddin was referring tonight when he spoke of some Australians 'putting too much pressure on ourselves'.

Ponting captained Johnson sympathetically, relieving him for an over after he had conceded four fours in six deliveries to Strauss, then bringing him back, rather than leave him brooding. They then stood side by side when Johnson returned at the Nursery End, Ponting with a solicitous hand in the small of his bowler's back while setting the field.

At each ball landing on line, Ponting and Clarke in the slips applauded above their heads. But there weren't anywhere near enough reasons to applaud, and Johnson fell into the trap of simply 'putting the ball there'—well, thereabouts anyway, for he lost 8 to 10 miles on the speed gun with no real improvement in accuracy. 'It just looked like he wasn't getting in the areas he wanted to,' said Strauss euphemistically. 'The right areas': that jargon du jour, where the individuals dematerialise and biography is reduced to geography. Here it showed its shortcomings: this was all about the man, not the place.

Under the circumstances, England should have done better. After Hauritz's maiming, Ponting had only three bowlers at his disposal—Hilfenhaus, Siddle and a combination of Johnson, Clarke and North adding up to a third. He manipulated them resourcefully. Johnson, however, is becoming Ponting's greatest potential headache, awkward to carry, but just as problematic to exclude. If Brett Lee were to recover in time for the Edgbaston Test, who would make way?

Johnson's role could need revising, his promotion to bellwether of Australia's attack having come so swiftly. Johnson might also be better off accepting that, with a slinging action such as his, there will be days he sprays the ball around. It was insouciance almost as much as speed that made Jeff Thomson so formidable: one never knew if an unplayable delivery was in the offing, because Thomson himself hardly knew.

Johnson seems to have come to need the validation of swing; having abruptly started bringing the ball back into right-handers in South Africa, he has grown discouraged by the absence of the effect here and in Cardiff. He should get over it. Consistent swing, of course, is a worthy aim, but better intermittent swing than predictable swing, especially at 90 miles per hour. The best advice would probably be the simplest: bowl fast, bowl full, and let the batsmen do the thinking.

For an attack with so little experience of English conditions—slopes, Duke balls and all—Australia's has so far punched above its weight. But raw-boned Hilfenhaus and rubicund Siddle, however willing, won't answer all Ponting's needs. Even if Johnson does not recover his best form, he has a contribution to make in spreading the work and wear. It takes a full XI, moreover, to properly celebrate a cricket success.

17 JULY

Day 2

Australia 1st innings 156–8 (NM Hauritz 3*, PM Siddle 3*, 49 overs)

'History is more or less bunk,' Henry Ford said famously. The Second Test is providing support for his view. For seventy-five years Australia has ruled Lord's, unbeaten, seemingly unbeatable, by its oldest opponent. Today Ricky Ponting's team disintegrated as noisily and abjectly as an old Tin Lizzie.

It was Ponting's fall that portended the collapse, which left Australia 70 runs short of avoiding the follow-on with only two wickets in hand. At each subsequent wicket, the camera tracked him to the balcony of the Australian dressing room, biding his time, biting his lip—as well he might have, given some of the headstrong strokes played. Hughes, Katich, Johnson, North and Haddin all fell to pull shots, the kind that in Cardiff produced spectacular boundaries but here a mix of drag-ons, strangles and skyers.

James Anderson's history against Australia, meanwhile, had been somewhat gruelling: four Test matches, seven wickets at 74.7. Today he reduced it to 51. In the last Ashes series he bowled two lengths and seemed to have lost a yard; in taking 4 for 36 here from seventeen overs, he looked more like the bowler who swung the ball consistently at 90 miles per hour at Chester-le-Street against the West Indies.

Not only was the past no guide to today, but the ease with which the batsmen were playing in mid-afternoon provided no hint of Australia's impending doom, having polished the last four English wickets off for 61. The leading indicator was the dismissal of Ponting, who found a bizarre, almost postmodern method of dismissal, being correctly given out by incorrect means.

It takes some explaining. The catch that Strauss pouched at first slip had come from Ponting's pad with no involvement of bat, contrary to umpire Koertzen's suspicions. Having not hit the bat, however, the ball was seen on replay to be destined to hit leg stump. Ponting was officially caught at slip because Koertzen failed to ask third umpire Nigel Llong whether the replay revealed the batsman to have hit the ball; all he did was check if it had carried.

Under the referral system to be phased into Test cricket at the end of this series, Ponting would probably have been given out lbw. But while justice was done, it was not seen to be done, for the only people who knew ought of the matter were television viewers aided by video slo-mo and Hawk-Eye. Ponting had to surmount his annoyance and disorientation quickly, for fifteen minutes later he was presenting his team to the Queen. The temptation was to reach for a speech balloon: 'My husband and I reckon that Rudi is a rubbish umpire too.'

Deprived of its copper-bottomed Ponting run guarantee, Australia's innings needed a new underwriting. Two rain breaks around an interlude of 21 balls posed a further challenge: concentration was disrupted, the pitch juiced up. Katich again proved his dependability and his idiosyncrasy, his little shuffle like a fencer's advance, his shots executed like jujitsu chops. Having made a century on his maiden first-class appearance at Lord's six years ago, he did not perhaps feel the same strain of unfamiliarity as his fellows. But he got himself out when the going was good, mishooking a long-hop to fine leg, as he had at Worcester, after adding 93 from 154 balls with Hussey. And from little things, big things grow.

Hussey's second Test fifty in his last fifteen innings contained some crisp drives, some succulent pulls and only one alarm; when 40, he zigged as a ball from Onions zagged, just clearing an unprotected off stump, Hilfenhaus having ended Strauss's entrenchment in a similar fashion with the day's second delivery. The Australian did not learn from his mistake, allowing Flintoff to hit the top of off unimpeded sixteen balls later. When Clarke was then neatly caught at short midwicket off the resuming Anderson, Australia had lost three for 8 in 25 deliveries, and the game's complexion had changed as completely as Michael Jackson's.

North had the misfortune to lose the bulk of the strike for a period, idling thirty-three minutes before dragging on what was only his fourteenth delivery, a slightly fretful pull. Johnson skyed his attempt at the same shot, Haddin miscued his, and the team that batted so deep at Sophia Gardens was suddenly out of its depth. Anderson aside, who bowled to a full length and consistent line, the English bowling was essentially serviceable rather than penetrative. Broad was mainly unthreatening. Flintoff touched 93 miles per hour again, although when he rose gingerly from a skid while fielding off his own bowling, he was the apprehensive focus of all eyes: hell, if he took a deep breath these days you'd fret about the wear and tear on his diaphragm. In the end, though, England's only concern was that Pietersen spent part of the last session off the field, replaced by MCC ground staff member Adam London, who sounded like a creature of Martin Amis's imagination but looked like Nigel Molesworth's nemesis Fotherington-Thomas.

The post-tea session, encompassing six Australian wickets for 69 from twenty overs, is only the third the tourists have clearly lost on tour, but it may be enough to send them behind in the series—an expensive lesson for this young team. Ford also observed that 'as we advance in life we learn the limits of our abilities'. That saying is getting a good run at Lord's too.

18 JULY

Day 3

England 2nd innings 311–6 (A Flintoff 30*, SCJ Broad 0*, 71.2 overs)

It was Spirit of Cricket Day at Lord's today. Children gambolled on the outfield during the luncheon adjournment. Two English batsmen walked for caught-behinds. Fat physiotherapists remained indoors. Of the general feelgood atmosphere, however, Ricky Ponting could not partake, as the errors of his batsmen on the second day were profited from by their rivals.

When rain ended a long day with seven overs remaining, Australia were 521 runs behind with four English wickets to fall and two days to play. Nothing is amiss with the pitch, but nor was there yesterday when Australia forfeited six wickets after tea. Andrew Strauss and his brains trust sat on their balcony like a conclave of cardinals, the whole ground awaiting any sign of a declaration—England's captain gave no indication of his intent, except to make his visitors suffer.

Australia's innings had expired fitfully in just over an hour, Siddle, Hauritz and Hilfenhaus adding 59 useful runs while not quite keeping their team's arrears to less than 200. Strauss then excited expectations of a follow-on by scampering off ahead of his teammates when the last wicket fell. In fact, Lord's provides no guide where the efficacy of this tactic is concerned. Strauss enforced successfully against the West Indies here in early May, but Sri Lanka (9 for 537 following on in 2006) and South Africa (3 for 393 in 2008) did not fold so obligingly. Today Strauss chose to bat again, and there was certainly no encouragement for Australia's bowlers in the remaining thirteen overs of the session, the captain and Cook adding 57 without loss.

After lunch, Hauritz caused some perplexities bowling into the rough from the Nursery End, dismissing Cook with one that barely turned, and Strauss with one that did. Ponting whisked him off for Hilfenhaus, hoping that the bowler who has been his most reliable would deepen the inroads with Siddle—a gambit that would have paid immediate dividends had Pietersen not been twice blessed on 10.

Still only coming half forward, Pietersen survived a pretty approximate lbw shout from Hilfenhaus, before stumbling awkwardly down the pitch. A straight throw from Ponting at second slip would have run him out by yards, and led to two weeks of Pietersen quotes that this is just the way he plays, that the hype doesn't bother him, that he's ready, huge and massive. Unluckily for the Australians, mercifully for jour-nalists, Ponting's aim was astray.

Ponting also had the chance to retard England's progress by holding a regulation edge from Bopara on 9. Misses don't come much more excruciating. The snick travelled so slowly that Ponting's fingers-up position became more suitable for prayer than catching; the cricket gods ignored him. As the ball came to rest in front of him, Ponting maintained his crouch, as if in supplication; the cricket gods laughed. Siddle, who bent over to be sick on the outfield yesterday morning, must have felt a familiar gagging reflex as he bent from the waist again.

Curious batting ensued. Pietersen can hardly have struggled more under such circumstances—a fat lead, a flat pitch, a deflated attack. He rehearsed more strokes than he played. His injured Achilles tendon restricted his footwork. Two short fielders in the covers and a short midwicket, a formation that kept him under control in Sydney thirty months ago, constrained his strokeplay. Twice he inside-edged past the stumps, bottom hand commandeering the bat; he almost toppled over essaying a sweep. He had been in more than two hours before finally he carved a couple of wide half-volleys through cover off Siddle. Otherwise, Hauritz was treated like Kumble, Hilfenhaus like Hadlee. This wasn't so much an innings as an identity crisis.

The only individual to make cricket appear more difficult in this game has been Pietersen's countryman, Rudi Koertzen, who as an umpire is a perfectly effective hat rack. In the last over before tea, Bopara (19) fetched Johnson from wide outside off to mid-on, Hauritz seeming to interpose his fingers beneath the falling ball. Koertzen could hardly have had a better view; umpire Doctrove could only have missed it at square leg had he been reading. Nonetheless, the phone-a-friend farce of the third umpire was repeated, and the detection of an infinitesimal doubt led to Bopara's reprieve. Ponting made enquiries—quite polite, by his standards. Hauritz looked keen to say something, but refrained, and finally had the last word, ending Bopara's subdued 136-minute stay just after tea. Pietersen and Collingwood spared Koertzen further embarrassment by walking for their caught-behinds.

England looked to be idling until Prior lived up to the vaunts of his batting with the most fluent strokeplay of the match, 61 from 42 balls, dragging Collingwood along in his slipstream during a twelve-over partnership of 86. Flintoff drove Johnson dismissively over cover to raise England's lead to 500 just before the rain. Across the big screen in front of the Tavern Stand was blazoned a friendly message: 'MCC wishes you a safe journey home and thanks you for coming to Lord's.' Ponting's homeward journey now looms as more dangerous than a week ago.

19 JULY

Day 4

Australia 2nd innings 313–5 (MJ Clarke 125*, BJ Haddin 80*, 86 overs)

Seventy-five years of history was never going to end with a whimper. And, fortunately, the bang looks like being of cricket rather than umpiring. Midway through the afternoon, fifth-day tickets for this Test match were hardly worth the price of their paper; if Michael Clarke and Brad Haddin survive the first hour tomorrow, they just might be worth their weight in gold.

In a kind of protracted re-run of Edgbaston 2005, where Australia advanced coolly on a target they'd hardly any right to approach, Clarke and Haddin used the last three hours of the fourth day to add a bright and sometimes even breezy 185 for the sixth wicket, putting Australia in sight of, if not quite in touch with, a remarkable Test victory. Australia need another 209 runs; England need a further five wickets. By most cricket calculations, England is way ahead. But the Lord's pitch is flatter than Nevada, and that oh-so-precious momentum, at least in the last hour of today, was Australia's.

For the first half of the day, after Strauss had declared overnight and set Australia 522 to win, the momentum was with England—and the umpires.

So far in this series, Flintoff has acted as a sort of media wind turbine, taking up an extraordinary amount of oxygen while generating relatively little energy. Today he showed why the oxygen has been worth it, pounding in from the Pavilion End like there was no tomorrow—as indeed, there hardly is.

Flintoff first followed a plan devised by the South Africans, who had some success against Katich bowling slightly wide, outside his eyeline. It worked a treat, Katich skewering to backward point, although it might have come to nought had umpire Koertzen been more vigilant about the front line: Flintoff's left foot had trespassed about 6 inches.

The 6 foot, 2 inch Flintoff then launched himself at the 5 foot, 6 inch Phillip Hughes, initiating the twenty year old in some old-fashioned Anglo-Saxon as he tested out his technique against the short ball at speeds consistently in excess of 90 miles per hour. It was stirring bowling, every ball pregnant with menace, even if Flintoff then called for physio Kirk Russell in order to remind us that these spells are not without cost.

Ponting punched his first offering from Anderson down the ground for four—usually a sign that his batting is in good order. Two balls later, Anderson retaliated, jamming Ponting's bottom hand against the handle—hard. Katich is a habitual leg-side perambulator between deliveries; Ponting not usually. Nor does Ponting commonly remove his gloves to examine a bowler's handiwork. Here he did both, his shoulders sagging as he did so, not with pain so much as resignation: that'd be right, he seemed to say. There was no call for the physio. Ponting has perhaps ceased to believe in them.

Hughes then edged low to Andrew Strauss—very low, so that the effort of Strauss to insinuate his fingers beneath the ball looked like one of those miniature cranes with which you grapple for candy in a seaside amusement parlour. Koertzen again turned to Doctrove, a sight that now looks as reassuring of imminent seriousness as a consultation between Mr Bean and Frank Spencer. The umpires had turned a low catch over to their video jockey Nigel Llong the day before; had they done so now, he would almost certainly have advised invoking the benefit of the doubt. They did not. With Ponting urging Hughes to stay, England insisting he go, and Hughes wandering round, looking as disoriented as Jamie Neale, Koertzen raised his finger, almost furtively, as though he knew he'd regret it later. If he doesn't, he should.

Ponting settled as if meaning to stay a while, swaying into two sumptuous hooks off Onions and constructing some portentously secure defensive strokes. Then, in Broad's fifth over, he stood tall to punch off the back foot without getting across and played on as the ball came back slightly down the slope. As if he couldn't take his leave fast enough, Australia's captain gave not a backward look.

Hussey did likewise, although in his case it was an act of commendable restraint. Swann's tenth ball spun sharply from the footmarks and was neatly pouched by Collingwood at slip. That Hussey's bat had been only roughly in the vicinity did not deflect Doctrove from deeming it a catch; the replay confirmed another gaffe. It was becoming harder to remember correct decisions than mistakes in this game. When North played Swann on, it seemed drably unambiguous, and it gave Swann 2 for 2 in 19 deliveries.

Clarke played exactly as one would expect a batsman of his quality to play against a workmanlike attack on a lifeless pitch, which was with great assurance and fluency. Which is not to underestimate his innings: as Mitchell Johnson has shown, it is a talent to be able to meet expectations. He let Flintoff bowl him one maiden, Swann another; otherwise he was unflaggingly enterprising, whether caressing through the covers or flicking off the legs, a blur between wickets, busy even between balls. England tried to starve him of scoring opportunities and partly succeeded: his second fifty took a dour 101 balls after the first arrived in a sparkling 58. Mind you, Strauss might have made the 90s a little harder for a batsman who fell nine runs short of a century here four years

ago—if they did not make it simple, Swann and Paul Collingwood barely made it complicated.

Haddin has been as secure with the bat as he has been
insecure with the gloves in this game, which is saying
something. He, too, put the pitch in perspective, trusting
the even bounce to play his signature back cut on several
occasions, as well as the usual array of muscular drives and
punches. Remarkably, the Clarke–Haddin combination was
only the second hundred partnership of the game, and the
first since its first wicket. It could hardly have come later.

This was cricket of an unostentatious competence. Even
the celebration of Clarke's first Test hundred in England was
subdued by modern standards—a kiss of the crest, a bit of
man-love, then back to business. As England took possession
of a new ball just before 6 p.m., Strauss convened a team
huddle to ginger up his colleagues, to no immediate avail:
the sixth-wicket partners negotiated the day's last six overs
in safety, accepting finally the offer of bad light. Tomorrow's
weather forecast is good; the cricket forecast isn't bad either.

20 JULY

Day 5

Australia 2nd innings 406 (107 overs)

John Dillinger was still on the lam when England last won at
Lord's against Australia. They have had to wait for Dillinger

to become the subject of a big-budget biopic for it to happen again. Australia was a similarly elusive quarry, compiling the highest score in the fourth innings of a Test at Lord's; England followed like G-Men, not always brilliantly, or even intelligently, but effectively enough.

The man of the match that finished at 12.45 p.m. was Andrew Flintoff, who ended his farewell Test appearance here with his longest spell of the game, ten overs, and only his third Test five-for, 5 for 92. He arrived a week ago looking fed up with cricket, having decided that this would be his final Test summer; he ended it looking disarmingly fit, and sounding suddenly refreshed, his complaint of 'a few twinges' as airy as the cowboy's proverbial deprecation: 'Just a flesh wound.'

For his part, Andrew Strauss confessed to a previous night's sleep 'a little bit disturbed' by the confidence with which Michael Clarke and Brad Haddin had held England yesterday. When Haddin perished without addition, the break for which England had toiled three hours, Collingwood's low catch at second slip was received with transparent thanks-giving. Apparently at this point, Flintoff told his skipper he could keep going until there were no more Australians left; Strauss was delighted to let him.

Clarke never retrieved his fluency of the previous day, when he had benefited from the freedom of little hope. Now he struggled to sustain the optimism. Finally he came skip-ping down the track to Swann, as he had done so often, but was hoodwinked by the slightly wider line; passing him on the full, the ball pitched and hit the top of off. Having made his best Ashes score, Clarke stooped as disconsolately as a batsman dismissed first ball.

While Flintoff burst the defences of Hauritz and Siddle, Johnson slightly redeemed his Test with a 62-ball half-century containing eight quality boundaries. When he first saw Johnson at Australia's cricket academy just over a decade ago, that shrewd judge John Inverarity took him for a batsman, noticing that he owned as pure a bat swing as anyone around; you see his point when Johnson's hands and hips swing through his shots, and a stroke with an abbreviated backlift and minimal follow-through streaks to the fence. The only chance Johnson gave was a return catch that almost took Swann's arm off; Swann had the nerve to vacate the cow corner boundary, and induced a fatal slog.

Both Strauss and Ricky Ponting handled the inevitable questions about umpiring with consummate diplomacy. Strauss' sincerely held line was that his catch of Hughes had been fair, and that he had 'bruised fingers' to prove it; Ponting deemed the adjudication as 'irrelevant now' and involving 'nothing we can change'.

All of which was very commendable. The unfortunate reality is that with two closely matched sides challenged to take twenty wickets in a game, umpiring is of disproportionate importance. Already there is a sense of foreboding about Edgbaston, where Rudi Koertzen is scheduled to make a return appearance, his 101st alongside Aleem Dar. To his 100th Test, he was the Dillinger: public enemy number one.

21 JULY
SECOND TEST

Three and a Half Men

At his standing-room-only press conference yesterday, Andrew Strauss was unsurprisingly full of praise for his team, which had played 'three and a half days' of really good Test cricket. It was a shrewd assessment. Tests actually last five days. England's 115-run win was a victory not of the excellent, but of the 'good enough', constructed around a first session of calm-browed batting and a sixth session of quality swing bowling in between quite a lot of grinding.

Strauss made a flinty century whose importance grew as the match progressed. His other key contribution was winning the toss, for it not only wrested for England the best batting conditions of the game but inflicted on Australia a kind of perfect bowling storm on the second day, bowlers freshened by four breaks (lunch, tea, two weather interruptions) making the most of a pitch freshened by rain. James Anderson looked twice the bowler he has, Andrew Flintoff the bowler he once was, and the same Australian batsmen who had murdered England in Cardiff succumbed to self-inflicted wounds, six wickets falling for 69.

From straits so dire, there was no stealing back, stoutly as Michael Clarke and Brad Haddin batted in their 185-run collaboration. It was rehabilitative for both. Clarke had made only three prior first-class hundreds in England, and had an unfulfilled tour four years ago; Haddin is bothering England with the bat, while also worrying Australia with his glovework. They showed what could be accomplished on a blameless surface that was probably at its best on the fourth day, their only failure being an inability to survive the first hour of the last morning. Had that initial thrust from Flintoff been withstood, there was not a lot of bowling to come.

Thus Strauss's well-founded circumspection. When the ball is not swinging, Flintoff looks his only bowler likely to break through, and who would back him to play all five Tests? Graeme Swann gave a first glimmer of his capabilities in the second innings here, but Stuart Broad again and Graham Onions made scant impression. Add to this list the England players who have yet to make an impression at all—Ravi Bopara, Monty Panesar, even Kevin Pietersen—and the room for improvement looms large.

For Ponting, there is the consolation that no Test he faces could ever be quite so hard as this one. His team had the worst of the conditions, considerably the worst of the umpiring, and by far the worst of the captious media and the boorish crowd, which made the captain its particular butt. He might take a leaf from the book of Warwick Armstrong, a matchwinner here for Australia a hundred years ago, who in his captaincy followed a simple rule never to read the newspapers—what Ponting does about radio, TV, websites, blogs, Facebook and Twitter, of course, is another matter.

This was always a series between two teams with little to separate them, and it still is, which imbues with unusual weight what in other contexts might be minor considerations: injuries, umpiring, weather, tosses. These are also teams not quite good enough to grasp an ascendancy, to maintain it and to dominate—which sets the stage for three further intriguing and watchable pursuits of the good enough.

21 JULY
SECOND TEST

The Eleventh Hour

Test teams enter matches these days amply prepared, intimately aware of their opponents' techniques and the anticipated conditions. Australia's order of battle for the Second Test at Lord's contained one notable omission: the start time of 11 a.m.

As Ricky Ponting's team drifted through the first session in an apparent fit of absent-mindedness, England's openers Strauss and Cook redeemed their failures in Cardiff with no fewer than twenty-two boundaries. Mitchell Johnson, in particular, perpetrated a spell of bowling that at a village cricket club would have entailed an insistence he refund the cost of the new ball. From the correlation of the lunch score of 0 for 126 with the eventual 115-run margin can be judged the cost of Australia's late start.

The strength of England's beginnings allowed them to drift at other stages—after tea on that first day, for instance, and on the third afternoon—without coming to harm too great. It isn't necessarily the number of sessions you win in a Test; it is by how far you win them. Australia's opening two hours were almost a plea of *nolo contendere*.

England's first Ashes victory at Lord's in four monarchs and fifteen prime ministers leaves Australia with several other issues to address, some of them makings of the original selection. On the face of it, Australia's batting has done the business: seven of their top eight have made half-centuries, five of them hundreds. But the exception is the highly rated Phillip Hughes and, while the squad contains a second keeper, there is no reserve opener. Australia are committed to persevering with Hughes, but he faces a runs-or-bust Test in Birmingham.

It is the Australian way, the conviction that talent will out, to persist with Johnson despite his match figures of 3 for 200; Ponting's post-Test remarks suggest that he remains a believer. The trouble is that the pitches can be expected to be more of the same, with nothing to make a fast bowler's sap rise. The risk is that a bowler blowing out in a four-man attack, as Johnson did at Lord's, asks much of the other three. All-rounder Shane Watson, now fit, or at least as close to it as he comes, could be seen as offering a reserve pace-bowling option at Edgbaston, especially if Marcus North's two soft dismissals at Lord's are held against him.

From being a trivial diversion, meanwhile, Australia's game against Northants beginning on Friday now looms almost as a sixth Test, with the other players in acute need of cricket being the seamer Stuart Clark and the all-rounder Andrew McDonald.

Thirty months ago, Clark looked as distinguishable from Glenn McGrath as a viola from a violin. Injuries and indispositions have worn away his keen edge, and he struggled palpably in the preliminary games. But his prior experience of Lord's would have been hugely useful to a callow attack, and it's hard to imagine that he would not have at least curtailed that boundary flow on the first day.

The other lesson Australia learned at Lord's is the degree to which they depend on their captain's stabilising influence. With him back in the pavilion, and the ball moving around, their batting was like a boat without a keel. Simon Katich and Mike Hussey showed their long-term county experience, but they are batsmen too naturally introspective to turn resistance into retribution.

Given that 2005 parallels are de rigueur, Australia can take encouragement from the fact that the team that lost first in 2005 won the series, after making good use of the hiatus following the Lord's Test to regroup—that team, of course, was England. It's not beyond Australia to do the same. But they had better make an early start.

22 JULY
RICKY PONTING

The Spirit Made Flesh

Like any good Test match, Lord's was great theatre. It was also passable pantomime, with Andrew Flintoff in fee-fi-fo-fum form, smelling the blood of an Aus-tray-lyun. Of course, every panto needs a villain, and one arrived ready-made in Ricky Ponting.

When his praise for England in a gracious post-match concession speech was applauded, Ponting smiled and said it was the first cheer he'd had in five days. He was wrong about that, having been cheered on the first day—when he misfielded. Otherwise, to be sure, he went about mostly to jeers and boos—from the crowd, from Marylebone Cricket Club members, from the English press, and increasingly from his own fickle media.

Ponting's problem is that the steady dwindling of his baggy green generation has left him the only Australian recognis-able to English audiences; thus he bears the brunt of all their peeves and prejudices about antipodean attitude and aggres-sion. The identification of Australians with no-beg-pardons cricket provokes bristling and cries of 'hypocrisy' when Ponting invokes the 'spirit of cricket', as he did at the end of the Cardiff Test in the context of England's time wasting.

Yet Ponting's remarks in Cardiff were actually the acme of restraint. He honestly admitted to some annoyance with the home team's tactics, then frankly dismissed them as insignificant. Strange that straight answers to straight questions could give such offence among the same constituency that always bemoans spin doctoring and doublespeak.

Ponting was the same at Lord's in the face of umpiring so execrable, and consistently favourable to his opponents, that regular counting to six seemed the best that could be hoped for: mild irritation on the spur of the moment, neither complaints nor excuses in the aftermath. Lord's, meanwhile, which preens itself as the locus classicus of the spirit of cricket, actually boos the best Australian Test batsman since Bradman—now *that's* hypocrisy.

The irony is that if a single player in the world could be regarded as a cricket traditionalist, even a bit of a reactionary, it is Ponting. He is a Test cricketer to the marrow, obsessed enough with the Ashes to have forgone the riches of the IPL before this series, so dedicated to its symbolism that he attends Test match press conferences in his whites and wearing his baggy green—unlike English players, who are studies in sponsor-friendly casual wear.

While Ponting does not publicly fetishise the cap like his predecessor Waugh, he privately honours it, maintaining the custom of Australian XIs presenting a united baggy green front in the first session of every Test match. A few years ago in Cape Town, noticing that Shane Warne had opted for the white floppy, he even pulled rank and brought Warne into line.

In the most recent of his surprisingly thoughtful tour diaries, Ponting professes a healthy scepticism about Twenty20, which he sardonically observes reminds him of 'schoolboy games when it was two or three stars in a side who scored all the runs and bowled all the overs'. He complains of the favouritism it shows straightforward hitters over more complete players, for he is universally admiring of good technique.

Elsewhere in the book, there is a fascinating account of a spell he faced in last year's Perth Test from India's Ishant Sharma—one from which Ponting emerged second-best.

Nonetheless, he concludes: 'It was great sport, and I was lucky to be part of it.' The form of words may be his ghost-writer's; the sentiments sound authentically Ponting's.

Above all, where decisions concerning low catches are concerned, Ponting and the Australians have striven, over many years but without success, against the tide in favour of yet more ineffective replay technology, promoting instead the idea that players accept one another's words. It's been greeted sceptically—admittedly, not without reason. But, in principle, what could be more in the spirit of cricket that MCC holds so dear?

Ponting's unpopularity is partly of his own making. He can be gruff. He has a temper. And where umpiring is concerned, he also has prior—far too much prior, and for which he was insufficiently chastised at the time. Now he is being judged in that light: he could ask an umpire to check his watch and detractors would construe it as flagrant disrespect for sundials.

Thus the mistaken conclusion of bullying taken by several commentators in the wake of Nathan Hauritz's almost certainly fair catch of Ravi Bopara a week ago, when Ponting was merely asking about 'the process' of the adjudication: a fair enquiry, seeing that it was as explicable as the Schleswig–Holstein Question.

Perceptions of Ponting and his Australians, however, are out of date. The captain felt harshly judged after last year's Sydney Test against India, but has worked hard to make amends; media perceptions often moving in arrears of

Heresy: Kevin Pietersen (69) struggled to impose himself at Sophia Gardens before finding quite the wrong way to make an impression, with a step-and-fetch sweep from wide of off-stump ballooning to short leg. As England lost momentum, Australia seized the advantage. *Getty Images*

FIRST TEST: CARDIFF

Orthodoxy: Nobody batted better all summer long than Ricky Ponting (150), his partnership of 227 for the second wicket with Simon Katich oozing concentration and endeavour, and reviving memories of the one-way Ashes traffic of the 1990s. *Getty Images*

Chaos: With time, and its wasting, of the essence, as the last English pair stemmed Australia's victory thrust, the appearances of substitute Bilal Shafayat and physiotherapist Steve McCaig would have smacked of sharp practice, had they not looked so clumsy.
Getty Images

Harmony: Jimmy Anderson and Monty Panesar achieved nothing with the ball at Cardiff, but everything with the bat that their countrymen hoped for. Nobody could have guessed how crucial their partnership would prove. *Getty Images*

Judgement: So many umpires, so much technology, and still the first-innings dismissal of Ricky Ponting at Lord's was a mess – a mess from which Australia never quite recovered, afterwards losing six for 69.   *Getty Images*

SECOND TEST: LORD'S

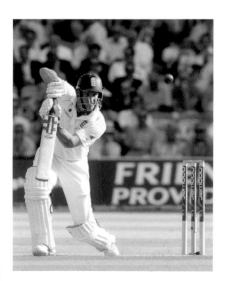

Leader: Andrew Strauss's first-day 161 in six hours, however, had already buried Australia, leaving the visitors to play catch-up cricket for the rest of the match. *Getty Images*

Heir: Nobody batted more fluently all summer long than Ponting's vice-captain Michael Clarke, his 136 at Lord's in more than five hours creating hope where none should have existed.   *Getty Images*

Fall: Taking the new ball for Australia at Lord's. Can there be a more sacred cricket trust? Mitchell Johnson's calamitous first day, conceding nineteen boundaries and setting England's opening pair on course to a 196-run partnership, betrayed it.
Getty Images

Promise: Flintoff's presumed successor, Stuart Broad, struggled with the mantle early in summer, but his catch to dismiss Simon Katich at fine leg on the second day was a crucial intervention.
Getty Images

Redemption: Having foreshadowed his retirement on Test eve, Andrew Flintoff's self-imposed challenge was to provide a performance worthy of the occasion. His five for 92, blowing away the last remnants of Australia's batting, fitted the bill.
Getty Images

Unplayable 1: Under traditional English cloud cover, James Anderson's traditional English swing in the Third Test at Edgbaston produced salvoes like this to detonate the stumps of Australia's stand-in stumper Graham Manou. *Getty Images*

THIRD TEST: EDGBASTON

Unplayable 2: England's hopes of a victory were then nourished by the perfect off-break from Graeme Swann to overthrow Ponting. It was a false dawn: Australia batted stubbornly, and Swann did not strike again for fifty overs. *Getty Images*

Low: In a collapse savouring of English cricket's baddest, oldest days, the home side capitulated for 102 and 263 in the Fourth Test at Headingley. Paul Collingwood was not the only batsman to find the pace too hot: England's numbers 3, 4 and 5 lasted 60 balls in the game for 16 runs. *Getty Images*

FOURTH TEST: HEADINGLEY

High: Lucky to retain his spot in the visiting side, Mitchell Johnson rediscovered his mojo with spells of wicked speed, and, belatedly, even some swing. Australia's win by an innings and 80 runs tied the series at 1–1. *Getty Images*

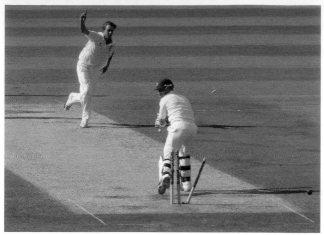

Delivery: Having improved with each Test, Stuart Broad delivered on his promise in the Fifth Test at the Oval, his spell of four for 8 in 21 first-innings deliveries including this devastating slower ball to york the dangerous Brad Haddin.
Getty Images

FIFTH TEST: THE OVAL

Pain: Reminded that they call it silly point for a reason, Ricky Ponting wore a cut lip for the rest of the game after taking a rebounding drive from Matt Prior. His other wounds were psychic.   *Getty Images*

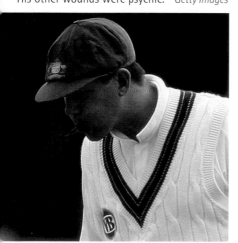

Euphoria: The second English centurion of summer was...only Englishish. South African-born Jonathan Trott's stern, controlled 118 built a match-winning lead for his new team, justifying his selection without pleasing everyone.   *Getty Images*

Almost: Ricky Ponting stood squarely between England and victory in the Fifth Test at the Oval, the equal of any bowler, but not quite of every fielder, being thrown out from mid-on - Andrew Flintoff's last Test hurrah. *Getty Images*

Not Quite: Graeme Swann's eight wickets, including the wicket of Michael Hussey that secured the Ashes, were celebrated with abandon, although the crucial spinner at the Oval was perhaps the one Australia did not select. *Getty Images*

At Last: After five and a half staunch hours, Hussey is caught at short leg; after thirty months, England regain the Ashes with a 197-run victory. *Getty Images*

reality, he is perhaps due more credit than he has received. The Australians' recent disciplinary record is hard to fault. Ponting delivered the last Sir Donald Bradman Oration; his erstwhile deputy Adam Gilchrist delivered the recent Cowdrey Lecture. Ponting's resolutions were sternly tested at Lord's, but he lost well, even courageously, at least by Hemingway's definition of courage as 'grace under pressure'.

Meanwhile, in the floridness of the commentaries and the boorishness of the booing classes, the true nature of his offence is revealed. Ponting dared to mention philosophies. It is the prerogative of cricket's privileged castes—its administrators, its commentariat and the members of its most exclusive club—to pontificate about those. Hands off our game, Tasmanian ruffian! In future, in the spirit of panto, Ponting will have to remember to look out behind him.

23 JULY
KEVIN PIETERSEN

We Need to Talk About Kevin

KP or not KP? That was a question as this series began, and now it has been answered. On the ground he took by storm four years ago, prancing like Whistlejacket, Kevin Pietersen cut a forlorn figure at Lord's, hobbling after the ball as would a particularly gouty laird. His 32 and 44 involved a lot of very hard yakka, as his Achilles tendon undermined his footwork.

Rest and rehabilitation were essential. All the same, he burnishes England's batting with a sheen of class they otherwise lack, and his loss will be felt.

It is hard not to feel a pang of sympathy for Pietersen at times. He is a magnet for criticism because his talent is so abundant, and because from this is imputed a messianic self-belief. In fact, Pietersen always sounds a little insecure to me, too urgently in need of praise. Marcus Trescothick, in his autobiography, described how England in his time encouraged Pietersen 'to feel there was nothing he could not do'. Trescothick would sit with him as Pietersen waited to bat 'and talk about the great innings he had played on previous occasions; that he was the only player alive who could play some of the shots he did'. As at Cardiff, such encouragement has not always been a blessing.

Five years into his Test career, Pietersen's replacement Ian Bell has flattered so far only to deceive. The batsman whom I would have preferred, in complete confidence that no selection so heretical could ever come to pass, is Mark Ramprakash, not only because his Ashes average is 42 versus Bell's 25, but because he is not such a known quantity to Ponting's team. A hundred first-class hundreds deserves a final chance for fulfilment; it would get the dancing crowd in too. Anything for a bit of free-to-air television coverage of the Ashes.

Part IV

THIRD TEST

Edgbaston, Birmingham
30 July–3 August 2009
Match drawn

Pitch 4U

Man is born free, but everywhere he is in chains—in Birmingham anyway, whose city centre in the twenty-first century has been devoured by the Bullring, a superconcentration of chain store outlets and franchises in which all sense of locality deserts you. From Debenhams and Tesco to Phones 4U and Foot Locker, with a starburst of Starbucks, a cluster of Costas, and the inevitable Subways and sub-Subways: Baguette World, Baguette Du Monde, Baguette Delicieux, Baguette Cetera (actually, I made that last one up, but it has a nice ring). You could be anywhere in the world, and it's possible that some visitors welcome the distraction from being in Birmingham.

At the art gallery there is an excellent exhibition of the life and works of Matthew Boulton, Enlightenment entrepreneur and industrial revolutionary, sometime associate of James Watt and Josiah Wedgwood, to remind the visitor that Birmingham on his death 200 years ago was a workshop to the world. Today the chief form of employment seems to be standing in the street holding signs pointing to the nearest Subway, the dark satanic sandwich mill of its day.

From Edgbaston, meanwhile, which has hosted sixteen draws in its last twenty first-class matches, the news is much the same: another regulation ECB belter, shorn of grass, coloured to a nice tint of straw, interchangeable with every other Test pitch in the country. Groundsman Steve Rouse called it 'low and slow', forecast 'bloody hard work for the bowlers', and described the resistance of the county's cricket director, Ashley Giles, to preparations that might have encouraged the bowlers further. Neither this nor the forecast rain bode well.

Recent evidence is in. How much more interesting was the Lord's Test on the second day when the pitch, lightly dappled with rain, suddenly started giving the bowlers some assistance? Yet administrators, it seems, would much rather a five-day draw than a three-day shootout in which the bowlers hold the upper hand; they would sooner risk resentful boredom than a refund. The trouble is that this hardly makes Test matches what is claimed of them: the most complete and thorough examination of the technique and temperament of a cricketer. If you produce chain store pitches, of uniform quality and character, then don't be surprised if they breed formulaic and mundane chain store Tests.

29 JULY
THIRD TEST

Short Change

The Ashes of 2009 will come at some stage to a hinge point or crunch moment—but not, one fancies, at Edgbaston, venue of the Third Test. Rain fell in such copious quantities this morning that one half expected to see an ark bobbing on the horizon. 'Sunny intervals' are forecast for Friday; otherwise, the slate-coloured skies are tipped to persist.

Persistence is the order of the day for Australia, and England too. For all the Australian agonies about Mitchell Johnson, he will almost certainly play. The selectors will hope that his bowling is more like his last three overs at Northants, when he was briefly quick and threatening, than his first pedestrian fifteen, when he was manhandled by second-division county batsmen. While Stuart Clark was the pick of the bowlers in that game, Peter Siddle enjoys his captain's confidence; Shane Watson didn't accomplish enough with the ball to sneak past Marcus North.

England have made a solitary forced change, local boy Ian Bell for decidedly non-local boy Kevin Pietersen, which again is an act of perseverance, Bell having been the reserve batsman in the first two Tests after four years of almost uninterrupted international tenure. Harnessing, like Johnson, considerable gifts to a diffident personality, he has never quite fulfilled the hopes harboured for him by Rodney Marsh during his years running England's cricket academy.

This subtle conservatism in modern selection is an outcome of the long period of Australian dominance in the Ashes, Australia's success being identified with long-term continuity of composition, and England striving to find a formula to emulate them. It's actually debatable how much Australian success *did* owe to continuity; it's arguable continuity arose from success. But it's striking how often these days the status quo is favoured, with an airy 'better-the-devil-you-know' justification.

What's seldom considered is how such a routine can contribute to the demoralisation of those excluded. For Clark, in particular, this tour must be becoming a purgatory. Andrew McDonald, who made a fair fist of his first few Tests against South Africa earlier this year, suddenly finds himself waiting for others to be injured. Brett Lee, already injured, must feel like he has donated his body to medical science—while still alive.

Where touring teams are concerned, the situation is compounded by the thinness of non-international cricket. Twenty years ago, Tim May could come to England, not play a Test, and still bowl 288 overs in ten first-class games. This year, Australia having played with XII at Hove and having scheduled a two-day game at Canterbury, there will be exactly seven days of first-class cricket outside the Test matches. Another Rodney Marsh, the footballer, put it well: 'The manager only has to keep eleven blokes happy—

the eleven blokes in the Second XI. The First XI are happy because they are in the First XI.'

At Edgbaston, mind you, the players may not see a great deal more action than the non-players. The Blotters—trucks on absorbent rollers designed to soak up surface water—spent today criss-crossing an outfield full of puddles, a complicated choreography that looked decidedly well rehearsed. Not for Warwickshire County Cricket Club the state-of-the-art drainage systems at Sophia Gardens and Lord's that allowed for play so soon after quite heavy precipitation. This ground is notorious for draining slowly, and had been drenched for days even before today's downpour.

Four years ago, Edgbaston was the venue for one of the best Test matches of modern times, its terraces seething with patriotic exhibitionism, their canopies intensifying the noise. The canopies now look useful for other reasons.

29 JULY
THIRD TEST

Birmingham Fault

'Ashes Countdown, 4 Pages of Previews' reads the banner above the fold on the front page of today's *Birmingham Post*. 'Plus Edgbaston Weather.' From where I sit, the halves of this headline seem on a collision course. When I paused to examine a weather map of Europe just now, England could actually not be seen at all beneath the cloudy pall. And even if the rain remits, the water table beneath Edgbaston will not fall in a hurry. The only cheerful sight at the ground today was a sign reading 'Caution: Ramps'. But then I remembered that England had picked Ian Bell.

Under the headline 'Let's Keep Tests in Brum', the *Post* also carries details of a mooted £32 million redevelopment of Edgbaston, increasing its capacity from 21 000 to 25 000 with a rebuilding of the southern side of the arena and the installation of floodlights. Not before time—although any ground would appear dour on a day like today, Edgbaston looks increasingly ramshackle, a drab and motley collection of stands, and a media centre that seats only eighty compared to almost a third more at Lord's. At Edgbaston, in fact, they still call it the 'press box'—an archaism so charming you half expect a seat to have been permanently allocated to Sir Neville Cardus.

The scheme has been resisted, the *Post* reports, by local 'campaigners', including the 'vocal' Selly Oak MP Lynne Jones, who complains: 'The problem is Warwickshire County Cricket Club has failed to adequately engage in dialogue with residents.' Heaven forfend that Warwickshire should fail to adequately engage in dialogue; it may lead to an insufficiency of satisfactory interface. It sounds like bollocks anyway: as I've found it, the ground is simply badly served by public transport. Birmingham, England's second most populous city, aspires to host the 2022 Commonwealth Games. Yet its cricket ground has palpably failed to keep pace with the legitimate expectations of patrons.

Bleak as it is at the best of times, Edgbaston will probably be bleaker these next few days. It is hard to foresee more than half a Test, which favours England, not just defending a series lead but keeping Andrew Flintoff in cotton wool. The sight of a rainy, windswept cricket ground will not entirely displease Andrew Strauss. For the rest of us, it's looking like a very long week.

30 JULY

Day 1

Australia 1st innings 126–1 (SR Watson 62*, RT Ponting 17*, 30 overs)

Shock exclusions are becoming an Australian Ashes routine at Birmingham. Four years ago it was Glenn McGrath; this morning it was Phillip Hughes; this afternoon Brad Haddin. 2005 was one for the early birds, McGrath taking his tumble during the Australian warm-up session around 9 a.m. This year the news came even earlier, although you needed to be a follower of Twitter account PH408, where Hughes had tweeted his unforeseen exclusion. The absence of Haddin then went unnoticed until after Australia's openers, an ersatz pairing of Simon Katich with Shane Watson, had begun a healthy partnership of 85.

JB Morton, aka Beachcomber, originated the classic definition of 'bombshell' as 'the exclusion of the cricketer' from a team—except that the Hughes bombshell detonated prematurely when the cricketer texted family and friends at home, perhaps including the publican of the Nambucca

Hotel, aka Bonzer's, where his local fan club have been gathering to cheer him on: 'Don't lay on any extra kegs mate!' Hughes's confirmatory tweet appeared at about 7.30 a.m. 'Disappointed not to be on the field with the lads today, will be supporting the guys, it's a BIG test match 4 us. Thanks 4 all the support!' Hughes having 1257 Twitter followers (only followers? Twits, surely), news of Watson's return to the colours spread speedily.

Times have changed. Remember the good old days when Australian cricketers only texted in relation to potential sexual assignations? For those who find Twitter as intelligible as Linear A, Hughes's historic tweet was at least an education. For the Australians, it was a considerable annoyance, as they were not required to divulge their team until half an hour before the scheduled start—a point in the day that kept receding because of the persistent rain and sodden turf, as though to exacerbate the embarrassment and elongate the analysis.

For all sorts of reasons, it looked a curious decision. Australia's selection panel, containing three distinguished openers (Andrew Hilditch, David Boon and Jamie Cox), chose a first-wicket pair of one reconfigured middle-order batsman (Katich) and an all-rounder with a Test average of less than 20 from eight Tests over four and a half years (Watson). Watson's average when opening for Queensland, moreover, is 4.7—interesting what you can find out when you have five or six hours with damn all to do.

The inconsistency is also obvious. Hughes fell victim to a leg-side strangle and a poor decision at Lord's; Johnson

bowled thirty-nine of the most shambolic overs imaginable—
yet it is the latter who has made the cut. By the close, with
Watson unbeaten on 62, the selectors could claim that their
gamble had paid off; it remains worth asking whether an
opportunity was not missed to bring Hughes into the series
at last.

Haddin, meanwhile, will not savour the sight of
Birmingham until it is in his rear-view mirror. Four years
ago, he rolled the ball that led McGrath into misadventure.
Today, as his captain was winning the toss and the teams
were undertaking their second warm-up of the day, he took
a blow to the fourth finger of his left hand, and had to accept
the probability, still to be confirmed, that it was broken.

England's Andrew Strauss would have been within his
rights to insist that Haddin played; as it was, he acceded
to an Australian request for Haddin's replacement by South
Australian Graham Manou. Michael Vaughan might have
been tougher. Strauss was perhaps confirming his pre-match
assertion that Australia is playing sans 'aura'.

After such off-field tribulations, the play that commenced
at 5 p.m. felt almost anticlimactic, particularly on a surface
rendered terribly slow by the unseasonal rain of the last
fortnight: 75 millimetres versus the usual 50 millimetres.
Anderson found no swing, Flintoff no direction, Broad no
pace, Onions no point. Watson could hardly have found a
more benign environment in which to begin his induction
as a Test opening batsman, and laid wood on the ball with
a resonant clop. He dealt with Onions, in particular, as he
would smash half-volleys from a bowling machine.

Swann came on at 0 for 84 after eighteen overs, already with a deep long-on, bowled a half-tracker, and by sod's law gained an lbw against Katich, essaying a pull shot. After another over Swann gave way to Anderson, whose second spell was as innocuous as the first. In the last forty-five minutes the ground was bathed in perfect sunshine—the crowd more than deserved it.

What a misery it has become, in fact, to be a spectator at Test matches in England, where tickets cost a king's ransom, if you can obtain them at all.

It was at the corresponding Ashes Test four years ago that mandatory security checks were introduced, in light of the thwarted attacks on the London Underground, rather like those at airports with metal detectors and body searches. Four years later the ritual has become mechanical, insulting and almost entirely pointless.

'Ticket! Ticket!' barked the warden at me as I arrived this morning, ignoring my journalist's lanyard. He then grunted at my bag and perfunctorily examined its contents, although I evaded the detect-o-wand when he was distracted by the crackle of his walkie-talkie. I could have smuggled in a kilo of cocaine.

Rounding the ground, I passed other entrances clustered with members of the security 'Green Team' in their posh uniform raincoats, resembling rookeries of phosphorescent penguins. A few were dealing brusquely with spectators; others seemed involved in no task more urgent than talking to one another.

The first session was then spent beneath an inky vault of sky that disgorged rain, almost eerily, every time one fantasised of cricket, causing umbrellas to mushroom as it topped up an already brimming water table. The mobile Blotters soaked up the obvious puddles on the outfield. The mobile punters soaked up the surplus alcohol in the bars and hospitality marquees.

Into them, meanwhile, the scoreboard dinned the ground's prohibitions on smoking and mobile phone usage, with penalties falling just short of transportation—although on such a day, transportation might well have appealed. Inspections followed when the rain relented: by the umpires at 2 p.m., by Andrew Strauss and his vice-captain Alastair Cook at 3 p.m., then the umpires again at 3.30 p.m., with Aleem Dar observed pushing a bail end-on-end into run-ups at the City End—hardly propitious for cricket. But mats were laid over the damp extremities of the square, and the thirty overs eventually bowled spared the ECB from coughing up a refund—twenty-five is the minimum.

Another threshold was not quite achieved. Ricky Ponting ended the day on 11 167 Test runs, eight short of passing Allan Border's Australian landmark, having survived into the Twitter age after starting his career at a time when people still thought email was pretty nifty. What a GR8 player. C U 2moro Pnta.

30 JULY
HUGHES v WATSON

Unnatural Selection

While few look like recalling this Edgbaston Test with much pleasure, four who might will be Australia's selectors. For much of this tour, wise judges have deplored a squad containing as many specialist keepers as openers. Within two hours on the first day both strategies were, if not vindicated, at least proven defensible.

The presence of a second keeper on tour is today seen as analogous to wearing a belt and braces—a needless precaution. The reasoning goes that a replacement stumper is only ever an air ticket away. Until the matter transference beam of *Star Trek* becomes reality, however, injuries like Brad Haddin's will require the presence of understudies like Graham Manou. One tick for the selectors—or what Cricket Australia, in these corporatist days, calls the NSP (National Selection Panel).

The other, more qualified tick was the replacement of Phillip Hughes at the top of the order by Shane Watson, who batted in some comfort through the two hours' play to reach his second Test fifty. You'd have had good odds on that a week ago.

Watson's name on the team sheet for the touring party a few months ago was asterisked 'subject to fitness'. It hardly needed saying; his entire career has been shadowed by the same caveat. Had he been a player even twenty years ago, it's doubtful he would have made it this far. There would not have been the medical resources and/or professional rewards available to maintain his involvement in the game. Even now, there's a sense that he's been persevered with as a pet project, that too much has been invested in him for it simply to be written off. Better players have had poorer deals.

The ratio of downtime to playing time has left its mark on him. His autograph is a rather painstaking imprint which dwells on the Ss in his Christian name and surname, suggesting something he has sweated over at length. Likewise his cricket. You sometimes sense when he is bowling that he has been given too much to remember, that as he returns to his mark he is ticking off a mental checklist. Nonetheless, he has always appeared a gifted and natural striker with a touch of Virender Sehwag's 'see ball, hit ball' philosophy.

Which is not to say that Watson has ever looked the stuff of which opening batsmen are routinely made. In fact, the decision to leave Hughes out looks very much like one taken in Australia rather than at Edgbaston, reflecting a change in the process of Australian tour selection over the last decade or so.

When Mark Taylor led the Australians in 1997 he was one of the selectors, alongside vice-captain Steve Waugh and coach Geoff Marsh—a none-too-happy triangle given the tensions over Taylor's form. Two years later in Antigua, with Australia unexpectedly trailing 1–2, it was Steve Waugh in the hot seat with Marsh and their then out-of-form vice-captain Shane Warne in the ejector seat—an arrangement even more tense, requiring the co-opting for Warne's omission of selector Allan Border, who happened to be on the scene chaperoning a group of tourists.

By 2001 the coach, then John Buchanan, had lost his vote, and captain and vice-captain were liaising with the chairman of selectors, then Trevor Hohns, back in Australia, although that still left Waugh with the unpleasant task of effectively ending Michael Slater's Test career. The system since has been for Australian teams abroad to be accompanied by a duty selector, who consults with captain and coach but reaches his own conclusions with colleagues in Australia.

That has some curious consequences, in that captain and coach are involved in selections on tour only in a consultative capacity, the members of the NSP being the only figures who vote. Thus, one suspects, the unintentionally misleading messages from Ponting and Nielsen this last week.

In his column for the *Australian*'s readers on 25 July, Ponting spoke glowingly of Hughes and his immediate prospects:

> There is a big challenge ahead of him, but he is a young kid who is willing to learn and to try different things. In view of the talent he's got, and the hunger he has for runs, I feel that he only needs half an hour in the middle and everything will click back into place.

Nielsen's last tour blog post, dated 30 July, gives no hint of a change of policy; on the contrary, it advocates continuity:

I believe he [Hughes] must refrain from drastically changing his technique or the way he goes about playing, rather ensure he does [those] things that he knows he can do well for as long as required … I believe it's important that he goes back to those things he's had success with in the past, plays with a positive mindset and body language and displays a real hunger for the challenge being thrown at him in this series.

No sense from Ponting that he lacked confidence that Hughes could withstand that half an hour in the middle, or from Nielsen that Hughes would be practising his positive mindset and body language in the nets, presumably working on his front-foot aura. Jamie Cox's view as duty selector, however, must have proven more persuasive, and Nielsen's press comments after day one—'He does need to go away and work at his game'—smacked of a subtle act of selectorial ventriloquism.

From the promotion of Watson and the non-selection of a reserve specialist opener for the tour, meanwhile, can be inferred a view among Andrew Hilditch and his colleagues that the game has changed. While we remain wedded to the stereotype of the opening batsman as a skilled player of fast bowling, physically brave and technically sound, the selectors may be suggesting that this view is obsolete: that because express pace is rare, and courage can be taken from a helmet and cuirass of padding, any half-decent batsman can do the job.

It's not a view without some logic. Frank Woolley began opening for Kent in the late stages of his career and found it famously congenial, commenting on how many more loose balls he received. Australia has done pretty well out of pressing middle-order batsmen into service as openers, David Boon, Justin Langer and Simon Katich following the trail blazed by Bob Simpson. For all that, I have always thought that a prerequisite of any successful opening batsman is a relish for the job—a pleasure in the contest, a security in the role. To Hughes this seems to come naturally. Watson may acquire it, but he doesn't have it yet; nor is it something in the selectors' gift.

31 JULY

Day 2

England 1st innings 116–2 (AJ Strauss 64*, IR Bell 26*, 36 overs)

Cricketers sometimes talk about having a 'bad day at the office'. For Australia, today was the proverbial go to work nursing the flu and a bad back, do two overtime shifts despite coming down with food poisoning at morning tea, and end the day by getting the sack. Worse, actually: they have to come back tomorrow. The only redeeming feature is that they might get to watch it rain.

Australia's day began about as badly as a day of cricket can. Strauss unexpectedly entrusted the first over from the City End to Graham Onions, the most military of mediums on the first day. Onions' first ball, delivered wicket-to-wicket at a zesty pace, struck the pads of a flat-footed Watson: plumb lbw. His second ball, similarly straight, was permitted to hit off by a perpendicular-batted, non-offering Hussey: plumb bowled, and if there isn't such a thing there should be. Hussey was lucky that the House of Lords yesterday rolled back the prohibition on assisted suicide.

After two balls the day was already transformed, as was Onions, who skimmed the ball off a pitch still soft beneath from the last fortnight's rains. Flintoff's bang-it-in methods were noticeably less effective, and Ponting picked him off through midwicket to become Australia's highest Test scorer. Having again been booed as he came out to bat yesterday, he did not milk the cheers now. Nor did he hang around when, trying to pull Onions, he found the ball rising above his ability to control the shot.

Australia would have plunged to 5 for 166 had Aleem Dar upheld Onions' lbw appeal against Michael Clarke, as he might have. They'd have been 5 for 176 had Flintoff held Clarke at second slip off Onions again, as he should have. But the introduction of James Anderson at the Pavilion End portended another redemption.

Innocuous the day before, Anderson now swung the ball consistently—not enormously, but enough. While he will bowl better for figures inferior to his day's return here of 5 for 35 from fourteen overs, he preyed successfully on Australian apprehensions about the moving ball, and also on some impatience.

Lucky with Dar, Clarke was not so lucky with Koertzen,

adjudged lbw as the ball shaped to miss leg stump; the hapless Johnson also fell foul of Koertzen, his lbw too high, although having played no stroke he forfeited grounds for complaint. With North edging a wide one to a full-stretch Prior, only the debutant Manou could feel himself genuinely beaten, playing inside a ball delivered from wide on the crease that bent away to hit what Duncan Fletcher refers to as T-O-O: top of off. It would have beaten Ponting; it might have defeated Bradman.

It really should not have been thus. The ease with which Australia's last two pairs added 60 in 71 minutes put the conditions, and the failures of their nominal betters, in some perspective. When Alastair Cook offered a timid edge to Siddle half an hour before tea, ten wickets had fallen in the day's play for 139 runs. Yet this was best explicable as the meeting of quite good bowling with some pretty indifferent batting: at the risk of repeating a well-worn sentiment, a risk the Barmy Army implies can be worth running, 2005 this is not.

After tea, Andrew Strauss added further perspective with the kind of cool, composed hand that Ponting must have fancied playing. Even the defensive strokes were constructed with intent and time to spare. Eleven boundaries included an on-drive off Johnson that travelled down the ground like an ice hockey puck.

So unrelieved was England's dominance that the Barmy Army even briefly changed allegiance. When the bowler responded to their chant of 'Mitchell Johnson-give-us-a-wave', he was rewarded, with a roughhouse irony, by choruses of

'Mitchell Johnson's Barmy Army'. It incited perhaps John-son's best spell for four months: a more positive captain than Ponting would have posted a short leg to catch Bell's hurried fend off the glove, while a better umpire than Koertzen would have adjudged Bell lbw, the ball destined for nothing except the bisection of off and middle.

Disappointingly, Hilfenhaus bowled perhaps his loosest spell since arriving in England, persuading Bopara to drag on, but obtaining little swing and giving up seven boundaries to an untroubled Strauss. It was a surprise when the batsmen accepted the light with nineteen overs remaining, England having had the kind of day in the office that they must have wished would go on forever. A hundred and forty-seven runs in arrears with eight wickets in hand, they will be eyeing the weather with more trepidation.

31 JULY
MIKE HUSSEY

Losing It

The Australian decline over the last eighteen months is tradi-tionally explained by reference to the men who aren't there: Warne, McGrath, Gilchrist, Hayden, Langer. It may be time to reconsider those who are, and no player has been a more reliable leading indicator of his team's travails than Michael Hussey.

Eighteen months ago, his Test average had mushroomed

to 80. Today, as his transformation from Mr Cricket to Mr Leave-It continued with a first-ball dismissal, it slumped to 52.91. The only enterprises to depreciate more completely than Hussey in that period have been nationalised.

It has happened by degrees, almost imperceptibly, with occasional reminders of past excellence to confuse the trend: Hussey looked untroubled at Lord's until, as here, leaving one he should have played. The stats, nonetheless, tell a tale. Test batsmen with 50-plus averages are seldom dropped, but such an instance might be in the offing. The strong, aura-oozing Australian teams of yore were able to carry one out-of-form batsman until his touch returned; this, as it seems popular to state like it is a discovery to rival DNA, is not such a team.

Worse than the dwindling average are the ways Hussey is finding to get out—or, it might be better to say, the ways he is not finding to stay in. He is in danger of becoming identified with the premeditated leave as once was Mike Gatting, with a gesture like ushering someone first through a door. And curiously, for a batsman whose technique was first held up as a glass of fashion, his stumps have started to take a beating.

A Test batsman of the front rank would normally count on being bowled only every so often. Of Ponting's 198 dismissals, for instance, just twenty-eight have been bowled—14 per cent. Of Hussey's fifty-nine Test dismissals, sixteen have been bowled—27 per cent. Something, then, is badly amiss. In cricket lingo, he has 'lost his off stump'—a quaint expression as, in Hussey's case, it is obviously still there, albeit increasingly lying on the ground.

Even when he was prospering, Hussey made an intriguing study. He is an unfailingly polite and personable young man; about his cricket, he has always struck one as broodingly earnest, a fervent apostle of the Australian strength-through-combination ethic, the chief chorister of the antipodean victory song 'Under the Southern Cross'.

Ryan Campbell tells a story of their opening the batting as juniors. Before they went out, Hussey handed Campbell a formal plan of their partnership, enumerating its objectives and methods in bullet points and key words. On occasion, Hussey still radiates a similar sense, of being so exhaustively prepared that he arrives at the crease having already played his innings in his mind.

Certainly, he is a great seeker of the reassurance of models. A natural right-hander, he began batting left-handed in childhood imitation of Allan Border. He is a disciple of the sports psychologist Sandy Gordon, observes a gospel of professionalism designed with goal-setter Vic Smith, and is close to the former Northants coach Bob Carter.

During a form trough in the mid-1990s, Hussey was so despondent about his batting for Western Australia that he wrote to Steve Waugh pleading for insights into 'mental toughness'—the psychological certification that bore Waugh's watermark. Waugh told Hussey he was too intense, which sounds like being scolded by Dylan Thomas for taking a dram too many, but Waugh himself became a better player as he grew into a broader man. Hussey took the advice and renounced the several superstitions he'd come obsessively to keep. The nature that had nurtured them has proven harder to alter. Although by the time of his Test debut he'd played 176 first-class games, he was so nervous that he suffered a kind of panic attack, his mind racing, his legs losing sensation.

Batsmen, too, tell you something about themselves when they get out. Viv Richards always left with his head held high: this was not a battle lost, merely deferred. Hussey seems to experience dismissal as a kind of professional death. A distraught look crosses his face, like someone has walked over his grave.

His experience today can be imagined. Having spent the last forty minutes of the first day in his pads, to no end, he would barely have finished his morning preparations before Watson's dismissal to Onions' first ball. Cricket is so full of pauses and longueurs—Ponting waited fifteen minutes before he faced his first ball yesterday—that the moments when you must hurry are doubly unsettling.

Hussey hustled out and, of course, hustled back, wheeling round and heading off without a backward look, as though he couldn't wait for the ordeal to end. The non-shot shot to which he succumbed was an attempt to slow things down, to get his bearings. Onions found the perfect riposte. A moment later, in repose, it would have seemed to Hussey like a bad dream.

The rest of the innings was indeed an Australian nightmare, turning a position of some substance into one of bedraggled confusion. Australia have persisted with Hussey at number four in order to keep their left-handers apart, but at the cost of his failures reverberating down the order, and the loss of wickets to the day's first two deliveries was like a shell detonating in a magazine. Ponting's Australian run record was swallowed up in the general disorder, and Haddin's no-nonsense strokes were badly missed.

These were more classically English conditions than, save for a session, prevailed at Lord's: cool, overcast, rain never seemingly far off but never quite coming. The bowling creases, too, were more secure than on day one, and Onions and Anderson ran in with confidence.

That, indeed, is what made Hussey's fall such a body blow. By dint of his seasons at Northants, Gloucestershire and Durham, he has played more cricket in such conditions than any other Australian, even his captain. One senses that Hussey knows it too—which will be making his failures twice burdensome to him.

Classically English conditions, in the form of rain, will probably save Australia here. Mike Hussey will have to save himself.

1 AUGUST

Day 3

No play

'I'm English,' says the comedian Bill Bailey by way of introduction. 'Thus I am conditioned to a life just short of pleasure.' Thus today's tidings from Edgbaston. A capacity crowd on a Test match Saturday at England's jolliest venue, with the home team on top, already 1-0 up in the series? Rain was inevitable.

Not just any old rain either, but the Sir Alec Bedser of rain: consistent, tireless, unrelenting. Rain so copious that water began reappearing on the ground from the brimming water table, the mobile Blotters spouting bow waves as they ploughed back and forth.

Patrons, nonetheless, remained in a remarkably hearty humour, lubricated by the various liquor outlets, sustained by a sense of shared ridiculousness. While the guests in their hospitality suites were grimly tuned in to golf tournaments and horseracing from other, sunnier climes, the punters outside remained in considerable numbers, even after the official abandonment at 2.40 p.m.

Songs were sung and impromptu entertainments conceived. Bob Willis and Jason Gillespie teamed up for a well-attended Q & A in the Vodafone enclosure, while Mike Gatting pulled pints of Marston's in the beer marquee. Andrew Flintoff wandered across the ground, sandshoes lapped by puddles, inviting photographs of Freddie walking on water. An air of village fair prevailed. There was even a game of cricket where batsmen dressed as Elvis and the Queen were surrounded by the Incredibles. They formed— what else?—an umbrella field.

One could, at a pinch, regard it as history being made: not for more than a decade had a day of Ashes cricket been surrendered entirely to rain. One could also see it as a comment on the peculiar nature of Test match time: the score was unchanged, but the game's dynamics irrevocably were.

England, comfortably ahead, have been outflanked by the elements—as, in fact, was always possible. With five sessions already lost, and further rain forecast for Monday, their seven for 77 before lunch yesterday looks like becoming a pleasingly symmetrical statistic rather than a match-winning performance. The proximity of the Rea to the Hollies Stand slows the drying of the ground here, and groundsman Steve Rouse will be hard-pressed to ready Edgbaston for a timely continuation. This looks like a Test match destined to finish just short of completion.

2 AUGUST

Day 4

Australia 2nd innings 88–2 (SR Watson 34*, MEK Hussey 18*, 28 overs)

A fourth-day stimulus package of ten wickets for 348 runs from 513 balls has recapitalised the Third Test at Edgbaston, but it will take a 98-over final day to determine if enough was done to remedy the damage rain inflicted on the first and third days. The sums still don't quite add up to a result: England retain a 25-run lead; Australia have eight wickets in reserve. But at least the markedly improved weather forecast is for cricket to play a greater role than climate tomorrow.

The scenario might have been more serious for the visitors had Andrew Strauss late in the day posted a short leg for Michael Hussey, facing a king pair. But short leg, as we are reminded incessantly, is an old-fashioned position, and bowler Graham Onions' scramble for the ballooning bat-pad chance fell just short. Australia, inches from 3 for 52 at that point, were 2 for 88 by the close with Hussey securely settled alongside Shane Watson. A useful lesson: following fashion can be expensive.

Commencing an hour late, today's cricket was a mixture of standards, some very good, some wretched, and even a bit of what when Aussies indulge in it in these parts is called 'sledging' and when their rivals respond is referred to as 'good-humoured byplay'. It would have pleased Shane Warne, who called this morning for a bit of 'in your face' from his countrymen; it brought rejoicings from the Barmy Army, who showed world-class stamina all the way to stumps at 7.30 p.m.

The day began with a fine display of stamina too. Bowling to a fuller length than on Friday, Hilfenhaus obtained decided swing, and duly ploughed a fourteen-over furrow at the City End. Strauss succumbed to a cramped cut after a quarter of an hour, and Australia had had the better of the abbreviated opening session when Collingwood played a careless drive on the stroke of lunch.

The Pavilion End proved a greater challenge to Ponting, Siddle beginning with a mix of histrionic appeals and far-flung short balls, one wide vanishing to fine leg for four, keeper Graham Manou watching it disappear helplessly, like a commuter who had just missed a bus. The answer proved to be Johnson, whose first spell of eight overs was a further improvement on his Friday improvement, marred only by a couple of no-balls and a stray delivery down the leg side which rebounded from Manou's outstretched glove for a couple of byes.

Ian Bell reached his half-century and reduced England's arrears to less than 100 with a neat leg glance for four, but he also lost momentum; off forty balls either side of this stroke, he managed only three scoring shots. As in the past, he seemed to lose touch with the game and slip into a kind of reverie of mannerisms—endless shadow strokeplay and Alec Stewart bat twirling. Although he had been in for two and a half hours, it wasn't altogether surprising when he played around Johnson, ending another unfulfilled, unfulfilling innings.

Flintoff's skirmish with Johnson pitted the Barmy Army's old favourite against its recently adopted antipodean son, the former responding to the latter's bouncers with some plain-spoken Lancastrian advice; Johnson cocked an ear, either feigning deafness or because he couldn't make out the accent.

Alongside diminutive substitute Phil Hughes at short leg, Flintoff loomed even larger than usual—it looked a little like a scene from a school's fathers and sons game. When Johnson and Hilfenhaus gave way to Watson and Siddle, the play took on that character too. Five fours in 17 balls spread good cheer through the terraces.

That Siddle's second spell of seven overs cost 47 needs no elaboration. Selector Merv Hughes's assertion that Watson was playing as a specialist batsman rather than as an all-rounder was also entirely corroborated: Watson approached the crease as though not quite sure what would eventuate, and it wasn't worth waiting for. Four years ago, he was routinely clocking nearly 90 miles per hour; the gym has had the same effect on him as anger has on Bruce Banner, but has taken the edge right off his pace.

Prior again justified his number six slot with strokes that broke one bat and warmed up another, then squandered his start with a miscued pull. Flintoff, in an unusually discriminating mind, levelled the scores with a nonchalant six to cow corner off Hauritz, confirmed a lead with a sweep for four that also raised his fifty, and appeared unassailable until an off-break glanced his glove gently on the way to slip. His first score of significance since Mohali last year, 74, contained eleven boundaries, saving him the evident labour of running.

The XL afternoon session, extended half an hour to make up lost time, yielded England 157 runs from a rather tardy 32.1 overs, with the Barmy Army's chants tracing England's ascendancy from 'If You're One–Nil Up/Stand Up', through 'Can We Play You/Can We Play You/Can We Play You Every Week?', to 'Are You Scotland/Are You Scotland/Are You Scotland in Disguise?'

When Johnson's twentieth over included 15 runs, the wicket of Swann to a slower ball from round the wicket and some salty interaction between the bowler, Swann and Broad, the chant of 'We Love You Mitchell/We Do' was struck up. It was tough love but may have done more good than harm. Johnson's figures were as unflattering here as they were flattering in the first two Tests, and he finally began directing more aggression out than in.

Broad kept England ticking over after tea with a 62-ball

half-century containing nine boundaries and at least as many fannings outside off stump. It will be enough for Broad to keep his place at Headingley, which may or may not be a good thing for England given his four wickets in this series for 307. With Swann carving about him effectively, Australia's deficit blew out to 113.

Australia's second innings began cautiously, almost furtively, Katich outscoring Watson, but soon came to harm. In Cardiff, just two Tests ago, but feeling like two years, Katich and Ponting batted seventy overs, grafting 239. Here they fell in consecutive overs, Katich fencing outside off at Onions, Ponting bowled through the gate.

It is a mark of Ponting's eminence as a Test batsman that his dismissal is celebrated with such abandon. At Edgbaston four years ago, his second-innings fall to Flintoff almost provoked an open-top bus parade. Today was much the same, Graeme Swann tearing towards extra cover as though he had nodded one in at Wembley, just refraining from pulling his shirt over his head. He had a lot to celebrate, the ball being one of those off-spinner's wet dreams, pitching right on the G spot of Mitchell Johnson's footmarks then piercing the gates of paradise.

Just for the moment, though, it was hard to take your eyes off Ponting: pensive, motionless, peering down at the pitch, lips drawn in, and finally retreating with a sigh. He had been welcomed by the now regulation boos, mixed for once with a ration of cheers. One wonders which is harder to take: the hostility or the sympathy? He did not remove his helmet as he took his leave; it was as though, at that moment, he just wanted his privacy. Harder still for him will be watching tomorrow, powerless to contribute. Swann, by contrast, will thrive on the memory of his wicket. A rummage in the records shows only one spinner to have hit Ponting's stumps as often as twice. Step forward ... Virender Sehwag.

As was England's assignment at The Oval four years ago, Australia will do the needful if they bat until about teatime tomorrow—and if this proves beyond them, they deserve to leave the Ashes behind. They are handicapped by the absence of Haddin, whose timing and temperament would have been invaluable. They are helped by knowing their task full well: the scale and nature of the necessary bailout is at least clear.

3 AUGUST

Day 5

Australia 2nd innings 375–5 (112.2 overs)

There was a brief security scare at Edgbaston today when West Midlands police investigated a hoax bomb threat, and a brief security scare in the Australian innings when their overnight batsmen fell before lunch with the team total just in credit. Both came to nought, the thin green-and-gold line of Michael Clarke and Marcus North placing the Test off limits to England with three and a half solid and dutiful hours of batting.

Their fifth-wicket partnership of 185 from 301 balls, concluding with Clarke's twelfth Test hundred, not only preserved the vital spark of this Ashes series, but kept England in the field ahead of an oncoming back-to-back Test match beginning on Friday. England's match-winner at Lord's, Andrew Flintoff, laboured here through thirty wicketless overs, which won't have enhanced his chances of opening the bowling at Headingley.

It was Flintoff to whom Strauss entrusted the day's opening sallies, and he started gamely, troubling Hussey from round the wicket and twice drawing him into errant pull shots. The sight of Hussey shouldering arms these days must send a tremor through the next man in too.

Flintoff also tried out on Watson the habit he has developed in this series of commencing the return to his mark with a few backward steps, eyes still fixed on the batsman, like a cowboy backing towards the doors of a saloon while keeping his hands near his six-guns. It was pure theatre, but the bowling accompanying it was not. One Flintoff lifter tattooed Watson's forearm; another took Watson in the solar plexus. Watson tucked into a couple of Swann full-pitches to reach his second fifty of the game, but, when Flintoff was relieved soon after, went too hard at his first ball from Anderson, thereby wasting his hard work.

Again Anderson commenced bowling under cloud cover, no more than half an hour after the ground had been bathed in sunshine. It's getting to the point where you wouldn't ask him to a barbecue. Clarke edged his first ball involuntarily to third man, and was opened up in Anderson's next over by a perfect outswinger.

The next wicket, however, was Hussey, and the next

wicket-taker, improbably, was Broad, not called for until the fiftieth over, and still to prove this summer that he is among the country's best four pace bowlers rather than a Hugo Boss clothes horse. His twelfth ball did nothing in particular, but nor did Hussey, playing while not quite committing. The batsman's best score all summer had neither saved the match for Australia nor quite resolved the questions about his place. Australia's lead at lunch was only 59, but England needed wickets soon after—which, as the sun returned, they failed to take.

After that initial seven-over spell, in fact, Flintoff was hardly to be seen, wearing an England cap rather than his usual sun hat as if to remain incognito. He crooked an ankle during his four tentative overs after lunch, rising gingerly and retiring soon after. From the attack that is: Test cricket has him for another three weeks.

The greatest disappointment of the day was Swann, glamour boy of the morning's back pages after his *coup de main* at Ponting's expense last night. His variations of length suggested someone feeling the pressure of the occasion; nor did he find from the footmarks quite the assistance anticipated. Clarke, beaten by him at Lord's, fought back particularly well, rocking right back to force shots through covers and point, then coming down the pitch to hit over the top. By the middle of the afternoon, with no further wickets down, England's outcricket suggested a team that was comfortable with and protective of its series lead. Strauss almost conjured a wicket from the part-time varieties of Bopara, but dropped Clarke (38) at short midwicket from a short-arm pull.

The closest England came to a breakthrough thereafter was when Swann hit Clarke (43) on the boot and Prior dived after the rebound from Clarke's shoulder. Clarke looked up to find English fielders in agitation and a puzzled-looking Koertzen—very possibly the last umpire one would wish to see under the circumstances. His level-headed colleague Aleem Dar counselled a clarifying call to third umpire Richard Kettleborough, and not out was the correct verdict. Soon after, Dar stepped smoothly in to placate Anderson, who had casually kicked a ball into North's pad, only to see it rebound away for a run. The 41-year-old Pakistani had as good a match as his 60-year-old South African partner had a bad one; if there were more umpires as sound, there would be no talk of referrals.

Around tea, the intensity rather left the contest, and even the Mexican waves grew a little ragged, especially that rather tricky counter-clockwise variation. As much competition was to be found among the rival spectators. A group of inventive Australians formed a beer snake of anaconda proportions, conveying it the length of the terraces. Varying the famous football chant 'You've Only Got One Song', the Barmy Army replied with 'You've Only Got One Snake'. That was asking for it: an alternative beer constrictor soon appeared on the opposite side of the ground, ferried by half a dozen men attired as chefs.

North reached his fifty from 90 balls in the second over of the second new ball, and Clarke his from 106 balls two overs later. They then picked up the pace, taking further toll of Swann and 17 from Bopara's first over when he resumed after tea, although the partnership was broken soon after when Anderson flung himself to his right in the gully to catch North. Clarke then made rather heavy weather of his last half-hour: at 92, a ball from Broad he missed cuffed off stump without removing a bail; at 96, he snicked Bopara to third slip Anderson but a no-ball had been called.

By this stage, the game had been surrendered to the statisticians, and Clarke marked his fiftieth Test by reaching his fourth Ashes hundred with his fourteenth boundary off what proved the game's last ball, Ponting declaring 262 runs ahead at 5.50 p.m. But the killer stat was 150: the overs lost to rain on the first and third days. Not that Australia will complain, acknowledging, like police, that anticlimax isn't always to be regretted.

4 AUGUST
ENGLAND

Atlas Shrugs

On the eve of the Edgbaston Test, the long-term forecast projected Monday going the way of Saturday, swamped by the deluge. The forecast then changed, giving England the chance to aim for victory; it might have been better for their prospects in the series had the rain fallen as first expected.

By the end of the hosts' unsuccessful victory thrust on Monday evening, all the members of their attack had done a heavy week's work: James Anderson (45 overs), Graham

Onions (36), Graeme Swann (33), to a lesser extent Stuart Broad (29), to a proportionally greater extent Andrew Flintoff (30), for not since Denis Compton has a cricketer's knee been of such national moment. In Flintoff's case, too, there's an ankle, hip and back to worry about as well.

As the long day waned in Birmingham, Marcus North swiped Swann high down the ground. Flintoff at mid-off turned like the *Queen Mary* and set off in pursuit at the pace of ... well ... a pedalo. The ball pitched, almost stopped, and just inched to the boundary. Flintoff's relief at being able to walk the rest of the way was palpable.

With the Fourth Test at Headingley beginning this Friday, there will be little time for recovery. All the king's horses and all the king's men will be trying to put Flintoff back together again, but from Andrew Strauss could be inferred that the prognosis is no better than it was for Humpty Dumpty.

'I think we can cope without him,' said England's captain, adding:

We've had to do it a number of times in the last two years, so it wouldn't be anything new to us. Generally the bowlers have stepped up when he hasn't played, but at the moment he's in great nick with both ball and bat, so we don't want to play without him if we can help it. You have to swing with the punches you get, and if [he's unfit] we've got a good enough squad to be able to deal with that.

Strauss professed to feeling positive about proceedings, the first-innings bowling of Anderson and Onions, in effectively harnessing the conditions, giving him special satisfaction. England's predicament, however, is that both bowlers are dependent on swing, and therefore on climate; Flintoff alone among his fellows, although wicketless here, has the pace and panache to work against the character of the conditions and the grain of the game.

Flintoff's batting—here seen to its best advantage in almost a year—would also be missed. Broad made runs and took wickets at Edgbaston, but in both instances after they really mattered: even if he and Flintoff both shave only every so often, Broad is hardly a like-for-like swap.

Nor did England, although they held the upper hand for much of the match, learn a great deal that had not already been acknowledged. Their batting again appeared dependent on Strauss; Bell, Bopara and Collingwood squandered starts. As at Cardiff, the slow bowling of Swann lacked first penetration, then direction.

If England have to permutate their XI, the possibilities for Headingley are either Steve Harmison, although he was troubled by blistered feet during Durham's nine-wicket win over Sussex today, or the horses-for-courses picks of Monty Panesar or Ryan Sidebottom. None will alter the balance of power in England's favour; at best their effect will be neutral.

The better of a draw and the retention of a 1–0 lead was a satisfactory result for the home team under the circumstances of the Edgbaston Test, with its incessant rain, fluctuating light and constant interruptions from both. This Australian team is certainly weak enough to lose the Ashes. The trouble is that England might not be quite strong enough to win them.

5 AUGUST
AUSTRALIA

Best of Five

If certain people, mainly journalists and exclusively Australians, had had their way in the 1990s, the Ashes of 2009 would already be over, with England triumphant. They were the members of a noisy lobby who campaigned through their columns for Australia and England to settle their cricket differences over three rather than five Tests, on the grounds that the older country was no longer strong enough to give the younger country a decent game.

With the teams closer to parity, they must be thankful that the Ashes has kept its five-instalment structure, for it not only provides an opportunity for Australia to fight back from its 0–1 series deficit, but the chance to see two further intriguing Tests between rivals able only briefly to get the better of one another.

A curiosity is that Australia leads this series in every sense but the scoreline. Australian batsmen have scored six centuries and eight half-centuries; Hilfenhaus, Siddle, Hauritz and even Johnson have at least ten wickets each.

For England, only Strauss has passed three figures, while eleven half-centuries have ended as such, and only Anderson has taken more than ten wickets, at a cost of 31.5. Flintoff, man of the match at Lord's, has managed one wicket for 221 elsewhere.

While distorted by Australia's batting beanfeast at Sophia Gardens, the statistics demonstrate why these next two Tests are such a blessing. Which is the better team needs to be determined by cricket's longest haul, a haul already exacting a toll: Pietersen petered out, Lee never started; Haddin is no certainty to play at Headingley, and Flintoff almost a certainty not to. It should not be settled by two sessions of swing bowling in favourable conditions.

There is a feeling that the continuation of the series favours Australia, ever so slightly, apart than for the obvious reason that it offers the chance of clawing back. It's probable we have seen the best of England, twice, when the weather was to their advantage. But we may not yet have seen the best of Australia, insofar as Mitchell Johnson only began turning the corner at Edgbaston, and neither Lee nor Clark have yet bowled an international ball in anger.

With the exception of their captain, England's top six sans Pietersen pose more questions than answers. Australia's batsmen, meanwhile, will arrive at Headingley with the lead back in their pencils after the second innings of the Third Test. Clarke is in irrepressible form; North and Watson have made good; Hussey's half-century was a curate's egg, but as the curate did not mind, nor probably will the selectors. The captain has averaged 21 since Cardiff, but will have fond memories of Leeds for the fine hundred he made there eight years ago.

There are now all sorts of reasons to anticipate drama in the Fourth Test. Strauss' approval for Australia's twelfth-hour selection of Graham Manou in Birmingham has made everyone a little less liverish, but back-to-back Test matches inevitably stretch endurance and patience. The Sydney Test in Australia, for instance, has become a flashpoint over the years because the players, umpires and even media are tired and cranky so soon after the Melbourne Test.

England used to boast of having a Headingley hoodoo on Australia—that is, until their rivals reamed them out there in 1989, 1993 and 1997. So stay tuned for a confrontation between two teams trying to sound a little more confident than they actually are—a confrontation for which we can already be thankful, and for which in the future we should be even more so.

6 AUGUST
FIELDING

Short Rations

Twenty-five days: it seems long enough to decide anything once and for all, except perhaps peace in the Middle East, or who is one's favourite character in *The Wire*. But after fifteen days the Ashes still seems almost impossibly tight, while also susceptible to even minor influences. Consider a matter of superficially minor significance: the role of short leg.

Next time you watch Shane Warne take his Test hat-trick at the MCG on 29 December 1994 with the wicket of Devon Malcolm, check where David Boon is standing to take the bat-pad chance: forward of the wicket at 45 degrees to the striker's stumps. That was the tradition into which we were born, the crouching Eknath Solkar or Mike Smith making even defensive strokes a dangerous speculation. Not today. For Australia Simon Katich and Phillip Hughes, and for England Ian Bell and Alastair Cook, have gone under helmets and on haunches to a position at least 7 to 10 feet square of the wicket on the on side—and so far have caught nothing save the bat-helmet chance from Pietersen in Cardiff.

Nobody seems interested in bat-pad catches any longer, and everyone is rather too concerned with the slog-sweep; the emphasis of the modern short leg, when he is posted at all, is on the catch taken from the face of the bat. This might already have had consequences in this series. Before lunch on the last day in Cardiff, Paul Collingwood (11) propped forward to Nathan Hauritz, and an inside edge rebounded to where a David Boon would have taken the chance easily. Katich was 2 feet too deep. Just short fell the ball; just short of a series lead fell Australia.

Mind you, at least Ponting had posted someone. On Sunday evening, Mike Hussey took guard on a king pair, facing his first-innings conqueror Graham Onions. He was bound to thrust forward, but the fielder who should have been at short leg was languishing at mid-on, as though for the famous Hussey on-drive which he doesn't play. Hussey, as an overanxious batsman is wont to do, plunged headlong at the line of the delivery, thick-edged onto the flap on his pad, and the ball hung in space long enough for Onions almost to bridge the distance from his follow-through. Hussey stood transfixed, his career flashing before his eyes, and survived by inches, smashing Onions' follow-up half-volley through mid-off to commence a rehabilitative half-century.

Australia might still have survived had a short leg been deputised, but Hussey would not be playing at Headingley. Any runs he makes henceforward, and they may be crucial in such a closely contested series, arise from that oversight of Strauss, and also Test match cricket's *The Wire*-like richness.

Part V

FOURTH TEST

Headingley, Leeds
7–9 August 2009
Australia won by an innings and 80 runs

Too Many to Mention

An embarrassment of riches, or a richness of potential embarrassments? No fewer than thirty cricketers were at Headingley today, each feeling he was a chance to fill one of twenty-two available places for tomorrow's Fourth Test.

All, moreover, will badly want to play in perhaps the decisive engagement of this fickle, fluctuating Ashes series. England lead 1–0 thanks to a solid win at Lord's, the better of a draw at Edgbaston, and considerably the worse of a draw at Sophia Gardens. But with ten further days of cricket ahead, Australia will feel thoroughly in contention, and maybe even confident.

All sixteen of Australia's tour party had something worth stretching for this afternoon, even second keeper Graham Manou, who deputised for injured Brad Haddin in Birmingham and awaits the success or failure of medical ministrations to Haddin here. Brett Lee has proclaimed his fitness, while Stuart Clark has never denied his; with Ben Hilfenhaus, Peter Siddle, Mitchell Johnson and Nathan Hauritz in possession, that leaves a quart of specialist bowlers to be squeezed into a pint pot of places.

Indications from Ricky Ponting are that Hauritz will be one exclusion. 'Historically the spinners have found it pretty difficult here,' he said, thinking probably of Shane Warne, whose three wickets cost 90 runs each. Where Warne failed, it is hard to see Hauritz succeeding. If the selectors lack the confidence to play Clark, meanwhile, his Test career must be considered over, ninety wickets at 22 or not: this is surely his ground.

England's squad of fourteen is constituted by their XI from Edgbaston augmented by reserve fast bowler Steve Harmison, reserve swing bowler Ryan Sidebottom and reserve batsman Jonathan Trott. All were on group Fredwatch this morning, along with a transfixed media, as Andrew Flintoff bowled gingerly in a black knee brace.

Their captain Andrew Strauss has said that the decision about Flintoff's inclusion will not be governed by 'emotion', which, if he's serious, suggests that one or more of the reserves will play. As time has passed, Flintoff's availability has looked less a matter of cricket selection and more like an episode of *I'm a Cricketer, Get Me Out of Here*. Will he? Won't he? Does he? Should he?

The availability on which England is really sweating, however, is weather. On the two seriously overcast days of the series, the second days at Lord's and Edgbaston, England have seemed to have twelve men in the field, taking seventeen wickets for 293, at 17.24 each. When either the sun has been out or the weather has been really cold, as in Cardiff, they have scavenged just nineteen wickets for 1265 runs at 65.66.

One reason Flintoff may not be overly missed here is that his wickets at Headingley cost 43 runs each. James Anderson pays 51, Stuart Broad 122; Sidebottom is the horses-for-courses pick, taking 8 for 86 here two years ago against the West Indies on what was his home ground before he moved to Trent Bridge.

Ashes cricket first came to Yorkshire in 1899. Headingley played host that initial summer but lost out three years later to Sheffield's Bramall Lane, notorious for its proximity to a colliery, which allegedly belched smoke only while the opposition were batting. England look like paying further for the decline of their country's coal industry, for Sheffield hasn't staged a Test match since and the forecast in Leeds is improving by the day—from which, just to confuse things, Harmison's rather than Sidebottom's selection can be inferred.

Overhead conditions will be especially important, because the pitch looks flat and featureless: having missed out on a share of the 2005 spoils, Headingley seems to be taking no chances on the Test lasting five days. After years when the future of Test matches in Yorkshire was said to be uncertain, a £21 million redevelopment is underway to transform England's darkest, most satanic ground into something more reminiscent of cricket than of collieries.

Headingley, accordingly, looks like a construction site. Considerable rebuilding impends. The same is true of the cricket teams of England and Australia.

6 AUGUST
FOURTH TEST

Terrace Housing

I first came to Headingley in 1985 to watch Australia play Yorkshire: Geoff Boycott's last game against antipodean opposition. My everlasting memory is of the broad Australian accents echoing round the largely empty ground as the fielders urged their bowlers on: 'Let's go, digger'; 'Get up him, mate'; 'Get quick now, Billy.' The ground was otherwise so quiet that I almost felt like a member of the team.

Headingley's reputation is now, of course, the very opposite, its Western Terrace being regarded as a sinkhole of spectator depravity. These days, in fact, it is called the West Stand, as if to generally try and raise the tone by force of nomenclature. It will take more than that, and Yorkshire County Cricket Club's chief executive Stuart Regan has mooted a variety of preventative measures, including 'spotters' at alcohol outlets, while the ECB's chairman Giles Clarke has written in the Test program that Ricky Ponting deserves 'the respect and courtesy' of the supporters who 'may never see his like again'.

Well, yes, although the enormous ECB billboard hanging at the Kirkstall Lane End exhorts fans to 'ROAR FOR ENGLAND', rather than whispering 'Respect and Courtesy: It's the New Black'. There is a distinction, of course, between supporting one's own team and denigrating one's opponents, but it inevitably blurs when you've partaken of the alcoholic product of the sponsors who pay large amounts of money to the ECB for the privilege of pouring it down your throat.

The chief victims of this hypocrisy have been the Barmy Army, large, identifiable, noisy and partisan, whose Billy Cooper has been banned from bringing his bugle to the game, as he was at the Gabba thirty months ago. Cooper, a professional musician, thus earns the right to describe himself as 'Banned on Two Continents'. It seems entirely wrong-headed to ban a symbol not of the Barmy Army's partisanship but of their organisation. For it is not the mass of spectators that is the problem: it is the out-of-control individual under no restraint who poses the most serious menace to players. The spectator who hurled abuse at Ricky Ponting as he came off after being dismissed at Edgbaston was not a member of the Barmy Army, but venting from the grandstand. And the most vulgar abuse heard from anywhere this summer emanated from the pavilion at Lord's.

All sorts of factors are at work here—too many to enumerate, really. You can decry the country's crumbling respect for traditional institutions. You can lament its binge-drinking culture. Yet it's no wonder that English spectators attend cricket matches with a determination to extract from the occasion the absolute maximum of enjoyment. They must pay absurd sums for tickets, sit in small and uncomfortable grounds, be soaked by merchandisers and franchisees, and get treated like dirt by security and ground staff (the Edgbaston crowd on the first day was kept in an appalling state of ignorance about the prospects of play while being harangued repeatedly about the ground's policy on mobile phones). It would drive you to drink if you weren't already halfway there.

7 AUGUST

Day 1

Australia 1st innings 196–4 (MJ Clarke 34*, MJ North 7*, 47 overs)

All week, commentators and columnists have wrung their hands over crowd misbehaviour and the general uncouthness of cricket's hoi polloi. England today found the answer. Folding for their lowest score in an Ashes Test at Headingley in 100 years, then plunging to a 94-run arrears, they left the hard core of patriots on the West Stand utterly dumbstruck.

Ricky Ponting was inevitably the subject of boos, but he might almost miss them now. 'Hopefully they'll boo me more because it will mean I've done well,' he said of the crowd on match eve, and he certainly gave them their opportunity, powering to 78 from 101 balls. It was a day, in fact, that Australia's captain will enjoy replaying in his mind, when even the toss was not a bad one to lose. He would have batted; Strauss did and, on a pitch that encouraged pace bowlers with bounce and sideways movement, watched his team dissolve.

It was a long day for both leaders, the whittling of thirty players at the ground to a final twenty-two before play being a madcap affair, rumour and hearsay commingling with injury and indisposition. The Official Secrets Act status of

Andrew Flintoff's knee was finally revoked, and the lurking suspicion that Brett Lee would not make the cut was also confirmed.

At various points before a delayed toss Michael Clarke, with a stomach complaint, and Matt Prior, with a back spasm, were also rumoured omissions; a distant Tim Ambrose was placed on stand-by for the latter. Brad Haddin, meanwhile, was included almost as abruptly as he was excluded at Edgbaston. It was like a game of selection bingo, although the winning combinations jointly accented pace, with Steve Harmison and Stuart Clark coming in for their first Tests of the summer.

At the pre-match preliminaries, Andrew Strauss shyly acknowledged that it had been 'a busy morning'; in his team's case, it had actually begun at 5 a.m., thanks to a malfunctioning fire alarm. He may have been feeling its effects when he took guard, for the Test's first ball, from Hilfenhaus, bent gently back in and struck a front pad that had barely budged. Late in a second innings, a tailender similarly adjacent might have been given out; Hawk-Eye suggested a point of impact roughly top of leg. But such decisions do not befall captains on the first ball of Tests, and Billy Bowden was duly impervious to a unanimous and prolonged entreaty.

In Siddle's second over, however, Strauss drove expansively at a wide one—the sort of shot against which he usually steels himself. Siddle hasn't looked comfortable bowling to left-handers on this tour, equivocating about coming round the wicket, for he loses a few knots when he does so. To be gifted with such a vital breakthrough from over the wicket so early was cause for great thanksgiving.

After Ravi Bopara tucked in against the West Indies in May, Andy Flower volunteered that he rated the 24-year-old 'very highly, talent-threshold wise'. Bopara has since looked increasingly vulnerable, batting-at-number-three-wise, and today departed so tamely as to call his actual place into question. The reproving glance he cast the pitch after gloving to gully was that of a batsman looking for excuses; batsmen at first-wicket-down must be prepared for pace and all its hazards.

It was when Clark bowled the thirteenth over that the visitors' grip really strengthened, reminding everyone, including his captain, why he was Australia's man of the series during the last Ashes skirmish. Johnson blasted out Bell between some wilder scatterings, but Clark levered out Collingwood, Cook and Broad without relieving the pressure for a moment, the batsmen scoring from only 14 of his 60 deliveries.

Siddle ended the innings with the pick of the figures, 5 for 21 in two spells from the Rugby Stand End, as England's last five batsmen smuggled just six runs through the field from 44 deliveries. There was no doubt, however, that Clark's was the critical stabilising influence—the influence that Australia have lacked all summer. It was the influence that England also palpably wanted for, once Anderson opened the bowling with two execrable half-trackers to Watson, both of which disappeared for four.

Harmison had Katich pocketed at a leg gully that Strauss had posted the ball before, but Ponting was swiftly underway, so swiftly that Australia's first fifty was raised in 39 deliveries, and they had accumulated as many boundaries as England within 35 minutes. 'Get him on the chopping board, Punter!' yelled a triumphal Australian voice—and there were a few of those today—when Onions joined the attack. Ponting coolly pulled for six, plundering 17 runs in the over.

For a batsman with relatively few recent runs to speak of, Ponting looked imperious, the master of his domain. When Watson played and missed a little loosely at Anderson, Ponting sauntered all the way down the pitch to issue further instructions; with centuries on his last two visits here, he was entitled to claim some expert knowledge.

At times, Harmison looked threatening. At others, his action looked more than ever like the Heimlich manoeuvre. He began his second spell with three looping long-hops, which Watson pulled, pulled and cut for four, then gave way after a second over conceding 10 runs. The bowling change precipitated England's only half-decent interlude of the day, when three wickets fell in 19 deliveries before Clarke and North consolidated.

Five minutes after stumps at 6.30 p.m., as though there had been a bomb alert evacuation, the ground was almost empty. Part of it may have been disgust: the crowd had seen only 81 overs in six and a half hours of cricket—an altogether dismal rate of progress. On the other hand, many would have felt they'd seen quite enough.

7 AUGUST
STUART CLARK

The Disciplinarian

Something unusual in this Ashes summer occurred in Stuart Clark's first over at Headingley today: he bowled a ball down the leg side, which cost Brad Haddin a bye. That, though, was unusual only for Clark. What was unusual for this series was that he acknowledged the lapse with a wave of his arm to the keeper.

Australia have wanted all summer for a bowler who understands line as a cardinal virtue, who strives above all for consistency, who tries to make batsmen play but is averse to surrendering easy runs off the pads—now they had him. He bowled the day's first maiden, didn't concede a first run until his 17th delivery, claimed his first wicket with his 21st—and not just Clark but every bowler around him benefited.

Australia celebrated the early fall of Andrew Strauss with an abandon that had little to do with the delivery, which was nondescript, something to do with the catch, an improbably clean pluck, and much to do with the perception of England's captain as the key wicket—a status magnified here by Flintoff's absence. The door was ajar; now to kick it in.

After eleven overs, Ponting made a double change, Clark and Johnson replacing Siddle and Hilfenhaus. Almost immediately, one was conscious of the attack's changed dynamics. While Australians imbue 'bowling in partnerships' with the same significance as 'batting in partnerships', there has been little evidence of it on this tour. Clark's steadiness here, however, was the perfect foil for Johnson's pace and prodigalities.

Rather than bartering runs for wickets, Ponting could concentrate fielders in the cordon, where five chances were eventually accepted, and maintain a short leg, who took two further catches. Rather than wondering where to hit their next boundary, as on the first morning at Lord's, batsmen were concerned about where their next run was to come from.

After an hour and a half, each Australian bowler had a wicket, an evenness of distribution reflecting the equality of contribution. Johnson was inevitably wild and woolly, but Clark tightened round the scoring like a tourniquet, until he was leading Australia off at lunch with figures of three for 7 from 41 deliveries.

The vital breakthrough was Alastair Cook, who made few errors until the last, falling for the fifth time to Clark in six meetings, an encounter rather like *The Itchy & Scratchy Show*: interesting enough but with consequences foreordained.

Clark finished with 3 for 18. Four of his ten overs were also maidens. Australia have struggled to bowl maidens on this tour almost as much as they have struggled to get batsmen out. In the three preceding Tests, Australia have achieved a maiden roughly once every six overs—especially unimpressive considering that almost a third of the total maidens were propelled on the last day in Cardiff when runs were unimportant. Glenn McGrath, for reference, achieved a maiden almost every third over. And McGrath springs readily to reference where Clark is concerned.

Clark first came into Australian selection calculations in England four years ago as a McGrath epigone, before outbowling the master down under thirty months ago. They have similar virtues: height, a tight wicket-to-wicket line, a strong wrist to regulate a perpendicular seam. There are few variations, but as Shane Warne once drolly observed: 'It's batsmen who worry about variations, not bowlers.'

In one respect, Clark clearly departs the McGrath mould. There is no chuntering, no glaring, and certainly no propensity for '5–0' predictions. On the contrary, he is disarmingly inscrutable; sometimes he might as well be bowling against a wall.

Once in a while, as he returns to his mark, an inner smile is outwardly expressed: there was a quizzical one today when he beat Graeme Swann's outside edge by the small matter of 18 inches. A certain Yorkshireman of yesteryear would have grumbled: ''Twere bludy well wasted on thee.'

Otherwise, Clark does the business with a less-is-more, let's-just-get-on-with-it,   we-all-know-what-we're-here-for lack of ostentation. Where Brett Lee proclaimed his fitness from the rooftops before this Test, for instance, Clark was determinedly low-key. 'I haven't got any massive statements; I'm just waiting for an opportunity ... Whether I get no wickets or 20 wickets, I just want to play.'

That calm is clearly contagious. The other beneficiary of Clark's penetration today was Siddle, able to attack England's elongated tail with a ball just a session old, and gaining 4 for 3 in 14 deliveries for his very minimal trouble.

The question inevitably will arise why Clark has waited so long for his chance here, when his experience, especially of Lord's as a former Middlesex player, would have been invaluable. One reason is that Clark was harshly judged at Hove for a lacklustre spell, after a prolonged absence following elbow surgery. Another is the commitment of his captain to the bowlers who served him so stoutly in South Africa: Johnson, Siddle and Hilfenhaus.

Ironically, Clark's opportunity finally arose because of a return to the selection precept Australia followed successfully during that very series: that of choosing your best four bowlers, regardless of pace, irrespective of balance.

Nathan Hauritz has done little wrong in England, not quite enough right. He has rescued Australia's over rate from the wretched and expensive depths it plumbed in India last year, but there is no doubt whom the home team's batsmen would prefer to face, and in the end the overs hardly mattered: England had to take the slack up, which they did with almost incorrigible slackness.

Australia's response was aggressive, with a touch of their old authority, and even pitilessness. When Australia was at its peak, errors stood out, and were swiftly atoned for. Stuart Clark remembers.

Day 2

England 2nd innings 82–5 (JM Anderson 0*, MJ Prior 4*, 32 overs)

Halfway through the second afternoon of the Fourth Test, a chant made familiar at Edgbaston was resumed on Headingley's West Stand: 'If You're One–Nil Up/Stand Up!' Say what you like about the Barmy Army, they know how to extract the maximum enjoyment from every situation. It will be 1–1 tomorrow, probably by lunch, after what shapes as the second-biggest Ashes beating to befall their country.

Five English wickets fell after tea this evening in 44 balls, 39 minutes and 20 runs—and it was every bit as hopeless, and as compelling, as it sounds. Andrew Strauss and Alastair Cook were going about their business unmolested, with fewer than ten overs remaining, when the former got his pad in the way of Hilfenhaus. To the next ball, Ravi Bopara did the same. The latter conspicuously tapped his pads with his bat, and the point of contact may have been half a smidgeon outside off stump. But Asad Rauf is an 'outer' with lbws, as he showed with decisions against Ponting and Hussey that some umpires would have shrunk from, so nobody can say they weren't warned.

Johnson, bowling fast and full, then had the honour of dismissing consecutive MBEs, Bell pouched easily at second slip, Collingwood torpedoed by a ball swinging in late. The selectors' patience, and Troy Cooley's coaching credentials, were further substantiated by a similar delivery going the other way to the left-handed and leaden-footed Cook. Johnson, a great deal more settled since he turned the new ball over to Hilfenhaus and Siddle, had taken three for 1 from 14 deliveries.

England still trail by 261 with five tail-end wickets remaining, unable to lose by as much as Walter Hammond's luckless team on a Brisbane sticky sixty-three years ago, but not destined to do all that much better. On present indications, you wouldn't back them for the Oval decider with bad money.

England were beaten quickly after having been overcome slowly, patient batting early setting the last session up. Michael Clarke was as Michael Clarke is: smooth, composed, pleasing to the eye, and extremely driven. Having had to bin a helmet the day before after stopping one from Harmison, he put the replacement in no jeopardy. His placement was constantly assured and his timing sometimes exquisite. One cover drive from Swann, for which he came twinkling down the pitch, hit the boundary board of Brit Insurance, the ECB's new sponsor, like a blow to corporate prestige.

On the brink of the exceedingly rare feat of achieving hundreds in three consecutive Ashes Tests, Clarke lost some fluency, bunted one from the leading edge into open territory on the off from Onions, then played all around his next ball, a subtle change of pace. It ended a partnership with Marcus North of 152 in 255 balls; there was no end, however, to North.

On the eve of this game, Ricky Ponting referred to

North only once, and that was in the context of his bowling, which he thought might be handy if Australia needed some overs of spin. It was an act of respect rather than disrespect: North is the kind of self-sufficient, set-and-forget cricketer whom captains instinctively value, particularly captains like Ponting, with a team so reliant on him.

The 30-year-old West Australian is such a self-effacing cricketer that when he caught Strauss one-handed at third slip yesterday it almost qualified as showboating by his standards, and when he reached three figures with a slog-sweep for six today it seemed like wanton exhibitionism. He has as few mannerisms as the high-strung Bell and Bopara have many; his cross-legged wait at the non-striker's end is as relaxed as a farmer leaning on his pitchfork.

But for a few late blows, his 110 in five and a half hours was all calm application, biding the ample time at Australia's disposal. Though he got off the mark as soon as he came in yesterday afternoon, fifteen overs later he was a somnolent 3 from 40 balls. Although there was more alacrity to his strokeplay today, the 14 in 6 balls with which he passed from 62 to 76 was runaway train stuff, and Clarke scored half as many again of their fifth-wicket stand.

England's attack looked, frankly, fagged, perhaps from the impact of back-to-back Tests, perhaps from the disillusionment of having to redeem the failures of their batsmen. Anderson began the day with a half-volley and a parabolic wide, and didn't really improve, his figures blowing out accordingly. His sixteenth over was a microcosm of his day. The first ball was defended; the second ball was driven back to the bowler, who stiffly failed to bend and instead kicked it away for two; the third was a play-and-miss; the fourth drew a good leg-side take from Prior; the fifth flew through third slip for four; the last was driven through mid-off, Onions bollocksing a straightforward save, to the boundary. Result: 10 runs from an over that should really have been a maiden.

Less impressive still was Swann, the fizz of whose wonderball to remove Ponting at Edgbaston has gone flat: he has bowled 264 deliveries without taking a wicket since, looking less likely to strike with each succeeding over. The last five of today cost 35, including a huge straight six from Stuart Clark.

Clark belted 32 from 22 balls, including consecutive sixes off Broad, much as he belted 39 from 23 balls, including consecutive sixes off Anderson, in Brisbane thirty months ago—although nobody in the England team seemed to remember that series. What am I talking about? *Nobody in England* seems to remember that series.

Otherwise, Broad had the best day possible for England, insofar as he (a) took 6 for 91, and (b) didn't bat, just. Mind you, the last four of his wickets came in four overs, and were not long after drowned out by the clatter of the collapse of his colleagues. He was, in a sense, hastening the inevitable— and the inevitable was coming hastily enough.

8 AUGUST
FOURTH TEST

Kiss Ass

The biggest cheer of the day at Headingley was for Giles Clarke—or at least, that's probably how he'll see it. In fact, the impromptu mid-afternoon roar was for Geoffrey Boycott, who was walking beside him round the Rugby Stand End. Now there's a conversation to have been the third part of at one's peril.

Both were on their way to the teatime presentation of caps symbolising Boycott's and Ian Botham's induction in the International Cricket Council Hall of Fame. Quite a conversation imaginable there too: 'Remember the day I ran you out in Christchurch, Boycs? My, how we laughed.'

Neither Boycott nor Botham actually donned their new bonnets, and careful observation in the former's case showed why: on the hatband of his rather spiffy boater, Boycott has had his autograph embroidered. That's Sir Geoffrey, already the foundation member of his own one-man hall of fame.

It was a crowded tea break, for, not two minutes later, proceedings were enlivened by an appearance from Kiss*, who, as any fule kno, continue to be scandalously excluded from the Rock'n'Roll Hall of Fame. Was the ICC about to claim Peter, Paul, Gene and Ace as their own? Alas, they had merely won the npower fancy dress award. Twenty-four gold

albums, 19 million records sold: what does a band have to do
to impress the selectors?

🏏

* As I didn't see the legendary Simmons tongue, it may
actually have been four punters dressed as Kiss. If so, my
compliments to them: they were very convincing.

9 AUGUST

Day 3

England 2nd innings 263 (61.3 overs)

They love their cricket in Yorkshire. You'd have said in pros-
pect that the third day of the Fourth Test at Headingley was
purely of academic interest, except that not even academics
would have spent their time so pointlessly: with England 261
runs from making Australia bat again, and only tailenders to
come, there might barely have been half an hour's play.

Yet if there was not a capacity crowd, it was close, and
they got their desserts, England's tail playing with such
improbable jauntiness under a welcoming sun that the occasion became almost festive. In due course, however, England
got their desserts too, sustaining a defeat by an innings and
80 runs at 2.05 p.m., the vigour of their batting's concluding
stages rather showing up the earlier petrification of numbers
three to five, with 16 runs to show for their combined six
innings. That the series is 1–1 seems a travesty of the teams'

relative positions going into the decisive Fifth Test at The Oval.

Anderson fell at once and Prior soon after when play resumed, the latter providing rival Haddin with his best catch of the tour, sprawling wide to his right to intercept an edge that would not have carried to first slip. Stuart Broad and Graeme Swann then united to hack and hoick 108 from 80 deliveries in 66 minutes, as incongruous as a sea shanty at a funeral.

Broad showed some pluck and some pedigree with a rousing 61 from 49 balls, being dropped thrice—at mid-off, deep mid-off and even deeper midwicket—amid some resounding drives and one effortless aerial flick to leg. After his six for 91, nobody could complain of England's perform-ance containing a Flintoff-shaped hole; it was in every other respect that the home team was lacking.

Swann, meanwhile, last night tweeted that there were '2 ways to view 2morrow', either as 'a hopeless cause or a chance for immortality'. In the end, he came to a third view, which was as the opportunity for a slog, and proved again that given width and length he can be a dangerous hitter. Taking 32 from two overs of Clark's, and reaching a maiden Ashes fifty with a top-edged six off his perennial adversary Siddle, it almost looked as though he was auditioning for the number three slot. He could do no worse than the incum-bent.

The other distraction of the morning session was the recurrent inability of the umpires to count to six, which rather threatens what, on present trends, looms as their last purpose in cricket; perhaps there will need to be a referral system for that as well. Billy Bowden confused himself by rescinding a call of five wides in favour of four byes, while Asad Rauf seemed simply to lose concentration, perhaps on account of having not yet given an lbw.

Broad finally holed out and Swann was belatedly holed up by some more accurate and shorter bowling, edging behind after lunch. Graham Onions then emerged in a suit of protective gear so enveloping that he might almost have been asked for ID. He quickly collected a pair, providing Mitchell Johnson with a fifth wicket, and probably batting for as long as it took him to get ready.

The post-match presentations were unenlightening except in tone, Ponting sounding confident, Strauss striving not to sound panicked, and settling for old faithfuls like 'not ideal' and 'didn't play as well as we could have', mixed with lots of 'obviously' and 'to be honest'. A lot was, indeed, obvious in this game, all of it very discouraging to England. As for The Oval, hope will sometimes earn you a happy day's cricket, but it doesn't win you many Test matches.

10 AUGUST
ENGLAND

We're All Doomed

Late on the second day of the Fourth Test at Headingley, the odds on an England victory officially hit 500 to 1. Such is the English affinity for nostalgia, one half expected a Head-ingley '81 battle cry: 'C'mon, let's give it some humpty.' But no, even the reserves of nostalgia had been exhausted. There truly was nothing to be extracted from this ruinous rout.

So what happened? The truth is that this Test was perfectly foreseeable as a continuation of broad-based Australian improvement since the first innings at Lord's, broken by a single poor day at Edgbaston, against a steadily weakening England, with home observers blind-sided by their obsessive preoccupation with Andrew Flintoff and all his works.

Australia finally fielded a formation optimal for the conditions, and when Strauss perished prematurely ... well ... dominoes have offered sterner resistance. England's attack then looked weary and woebegone, partly from the endeavours at Edgbaston, partly from the paltry total they were defending, and, if you believe Justin Langer, partly from *le vice anglais* of chucking in the towel, bucket and sponge when things go wrong.

The *Sunday Telegraph* chose a cruelly apposite day to publish a 'dossier' written by Langer and circulated among his former teammates and successors before the First Test. Judgements that might have jarred a little after Lord's seemed to fit very exactly in the circumstances of an innings-and-80-run defeat:

> They [England] are the best in the world at tapering
> off quickly when things go a bit flat for them. This
> is also a time when most of them make all sorts of
> excuses and start looking around to point the finger

at everyone else. It is a classic English trait. They love being comfortable. Take them out of their comfort zone and they don't like it for a second.

It was difficult, for instance, to dispute Langer's pithy assessment of Jimmy Anderson, so penetrative when skies are overcast, but revealed at Headingley to have a vampire-like susceptibility to sunlight: 'Can swing the ball well but again can be a bit of a pussy if he is worn down. His body language could be detrimental to them if we get on top of him early.' Certainly, Michael Vaughan's defence of Anderson didn't exactly sound like a resounding endorsement: 'I think describing James Anderson as a "pussy" is very harsh but it goes to show that there are no secrets in international cricket.' Cheers Vaughany.

Whether Langer is right or wrong in his views, the leaking of the dossier to an English media reverting to its default masochism setting is probably more significant than the contents. In 2001, a dossier prepared for the Australians by their coach John Buchanan found its way into the papers, where it was pored over like the plans of a top-secret superweapon, when all it revealed was Buchanan's flair for pop philosophy.

At the post-match press conference, Ponting took particular pleasure in the story on the *Telegraph*'s facing page calling for the rehabilitation of 39-year-old Mark Ramprakash for the Oval Test: he thought it betrayed panic. It may well be a sensible expedient, given Ramprakash's records against Australia and on his home ground, but Australians thrive on what they perceive as signs of panic, and weakness in general. They have had a rich variety to savour here.

In this respect, too, Australians are made of sterner stuff. If a former English player vouchsafed in a dossier then made public that Australia were 'best in the world at tapering off quickly', the headlines in newspapers down under would be: 'Pom admits: Aussies "best in the world".' Where cricket is concerned, Australians haven't been ones for nostalgia— and, frankly, they haven't had to be.

11 AUGUST
AUSTRALIA

The Past Is Not Another Country

For much of this tour, Ricky Ponting's Australians have been burdened by comparisons with the past, with the general consensus being that there is perhaps more talent among the former Australian greats following the tour (Shane Warne, Matthew Hayden, Merv Hughes, Jason Gillespie) than those on the field at any particular time. When Andrew Strauss was induced to comment that the current team lacked 'aura', indeed, he was merely expressing what was widely thought, for which the media thanked him by extracting from it a week of soundalike headlines.

The team's win at Headingley, however, as well as being a kind of DIY 'aura' kit, deserves at least semi-legendary status in the annals of Australian achievement—if not up with Port

Elizabeth '97 and Adelaide '06, then alongside Manchester '97 and Hobart '99. Australia didn't, perhaps, play exactly like the number one team in the world, but they certainly made England look overpromoted at number five.

At the press conference afterwards, Ponting sat beside man of the match Marcus North. After a while, it was almost like North had come in by mistake, having taken a wrong turn on the way to the nearby lavatories, and was too embarrassed to leave. Every question was directed at the captain, and rightly. Like Saint Sebastian, he has stood still taking the arrows on this tour: from the crowds, from the media and from past Aussie greats as well as from his opponents. Now England were the targets and, without gloating, he didn't mind sharing his pleasure.

With all due respect to North, Ponting would have been a more fitting recipient of the individual award. His innings here was reminiscent of Allan Border's on this same ground twenty years ago, when he took England's attack on at a hinge point in the innings: brash, bristling, brimming with shots, full of intent.

Ponting's first ball from Harmison cut him in half; to his second, well wide of off stump, he played a pull and missed. It was, again, a clinch moment. England had taken an early wicket on a pitch that they had made to seem fuller of demons than *The Amityville Horror*. Ponting, too, had perished to the pull shot at Edgbaston, having otherwise played his pet stroke relatively little on tour.

What happened next was worth watching. Ponting didn't abort the shot. He took the bat to the end of its follow-through, held the pose momentarily, then rehearsed the shot once more. Once bitten, he would not permit even the pretence of shyness. We were to see the pull again and again, as Ponting seized on every short ball—and there were many.

His 78 set the tone of Australia's reply, and also the standard: a guillotine-clean back cut and whipcrack back-foot cover drive off Anderson were shots for the ages. But it was his trademark pull, played with the same panache as Ian Chappell tackled the hook at Lord's in 1972, that proclaimed Ponting's resolution. By the time he was out, Australia had a lead which North and Clarke could then extend.

Others will have reason to look back on this game with pleasure. The best figures of the first innings were returned by Siddle, whose robust, repeatable action and crocodilian smile have become reassuringly familiar features of the Australian attack. The best figures of the second fell to Mitchell Johnson, who appears to have grasped the truth about the perfect being the enemy of the good since settling into the role of first-change bowler.

It was Stuart Clark in the first innings, however, who most exactly fulfilled his mission specifications, and Ponting was a noticeably more aggressive leader for the presence in his bowling ranks of such an accomplished restrictor of runs, and also a fourth survivor of Australia's last Ashes campaign. From the past, then, had come a blessing, further evidence of the complete turnabout this Ashes tour has undergone in the space of a week.

12 AUGUST
HEADINGLEY

A Room with a View

So farewell, then, Headingley: by the time I return, if the redevelopment plans proceed, this venue will look very different, which will not be entirely unregretted. Headingley is decidedly unusual among modern grounds in that the players and press are in close proximity. You thread your way to the lavatories past the doors of the home and away dressing rooms, while players can watch proceedings from a variety of vantage points, including on a platform right next to the press box. Michael Hussey awaited his innings there on the second day, jumping in and out of his seat to stretch and to run on the spot, the scrape of his spikes mingling with the gentle pocketa-pocketa of laptop keys. Slow to get started this summer, he was clearly intent on being switched on for his first ball.

For this closeness, journalists pay a price. The roof of the press box is so low as to render the sky invisible, and I've watched this game with my view partly obscured by a pillar. But there is something weirdly compelling about walking past the figure of Brad Haddin in a plastic chair awaiting his turn to bat, much as a club player might—except perhaps for the absence of a cigarette dangling from his lips. The accessibility of the area has some interesting consequences too. The previous Ashes Test at Headingley, if you recall, was enlivened by a prank perpetrated by one Karl Power, who, attired as an England batsman, hid out in the downstairs lavatory then threaded his way to the centre. Given that England's numbers three to five in this Test were dismissed by six of the 60 deliveries they faced, a similar impersonation might have occurred without anyone noticing.

The players won't be sorry to be separately quartered in future; on the contrary, they'll welcome the extension of the *cordon sanitaire* they enjoy elsewhere. But it will be a loss for us. The players are apt to remind us that they are only flesh and blood; it is no bad thing for this to be incidentally and involuntarily evidenced by contact, however fleeting.

Part VI

FIFTH TEST

Kennington Oval, London
20–23 July 2009
England won by 197 runs

13 AUGUST
MARK RAMPRAKASH

The Comeback Kid?

Mark Ramprakash—man or myth? The matter of his selection for The Oval is one on which most everyone in English cricket has an opinion, with wise advocates in both corners, including two friends of mine whose opinions I respect: Scyld Berry is pro, Michael Atherton against. As I argued for Ramprakash's selection at Edgbaston, you'd expect me to side with Berry now; actually, I'm not so sure.

The context of Ramprakash's inclusion for the Third Test would have been as a straight swap for Kevin Pietersen in an order that otherwise was demanding no change in a team that then led 1–0. The context of his choice for The Oval would be as a national saviour, supported by the influential ballroom dancing lobby, promoted for the purposes of one-off deliverance.

Everyone is enamoured of the romance of the comeback, but the English are particularly so: see Wilf Rhodes in 1926, Cyril Washbrook in 1956, Colin Cowdrey in 1974–75. But comebacks most often fail. Cowdrey, genteel, parfit knight, was flown out of an English winter after a three-year career hiatus to face Lillee and Thomson. The team itself favoured the inclusion of Basil D'Oliveira; the Aussies expected Barry Wood; either might have been better. Cowdrey's was a brave, honourable and futile gesture. He averaged 18. Most English comebacks have ended like that of Chris Tavaré twenty years ago: recalled for one Test after five years on the sidelines, dismissed for 2 and never heard of again.

So context matters. The reason most comebacks fail is that they are desperate measures in the shadow of defeat, in weak teams that have run short of other options. Rhodes and Washbrook were exceptions in result having been exceptions in context, coming into good teams on the brink of great deeds. I'd still like to see Ramps at The Oval: curiosity overwhelms me. But if it's thought the best solution in the circumstances, I'll be surprised.

13 AUGUST
MATTHEW HAYDEN

Meet the New Boss

In other recall news, Matthew Hayden is to join the board of Cricket Australia, bringing the experience of 103 Tests and numberless unintelligible press conferences. 'The game is definitely at the coalface of anticipated change,' he says, coalfaces being well known for their state of constant flux. 'What I can bring to the table is a real currency and a slightly more contemporary style of looking at the way cricket and the business of cricket is managed and maintained.' Real currency? Is he talking about his IPL moolah? How big a table will be required?

What Haydos certainly brings is a certain swagger, now corporate rather than cricket:

> Strategically it's really important to recognise that iconic series such as the Ashes can never be removed, and in fact need to be protected and maintained, throughout the cricketing landscape. At a time when the market is looking to find new ways to engage our sport I think it's also really important to go on a journey and go on a debate and recognise that we have got something very special in the creation of franchise cricket and the globalisation of those brands.

Giles Clarke had better look to his laurels. Haydos sounds like he could management-babble anyone under the table.

14 AUGUST
ENGLAND

Losing the Thread

'Winning isn't everything; it's the only thing.' Commonly attributed to Vince Lombardi, it ranks as one of sport's top ten desk calendar wisdoms. It is also decidedly unhelpful.

The problem is not the moral reprehensibility that some find in its consignment of all but winners to the outer darkness. It's that it treats defeat as straightforward oblivion, in which nothing is achieved, nobody is improved, and everyone associated is condemned—rather like the state in which English cricket has languished since the Headingley Test.

Facing the press afterwards, Ricky Ponting struggled to keep a straight face as he mused on how long a week in cricket can be. Before the game, it was all 'glory-glory-Ashes-coming-home'; during and after, the failures were not simply of the English cricket team, but of English cricket, and fundamentally of England too.

Particularly pored over were the remarks of Justin Langer in his confidential-no-longer 'dossier', which a host of past England greats rushed to endorse. It contained prophecies the media hastened to fulfil—such as that the habit of excuse making and finger pointing is 'a classic English trait'.

All rather puzzling for an Australian: one might have expected England to be better at losing, what with all that practice. Actually, the English used to be famous for grace under pressure, phlegmatism under fire. The orgy of self-recrimination since Leeds appears to reflect rather more recent developments in national character: a seeming relish, even a masochistic hankering, for pessimism, for panic, for analysis to the point of paralysis.

Even the cathartic catchcry of 'sack-this-lot-and-pick-a-bunch-of-kids' sounds a thing of the past. These days, it appears, the public figure ripest for ridicule is the individual who fails to embrace disaster, so out of touch as to have missed the obvious unfolding calamity, like Jim Callaghan thirty years ago, his remarks immortally condensed as: 'Crisis? What crisis?'

To be fair, one must never mistake the effusions of the media for a prevailing popular sentiment. On the other hand, from the industrial quantities of dismay can be inferred a belief in a market receptive to it. Yet for all the unflattering comparisons with Australia in which England is indulging, it wasn't so long ago that Australia was losing Tests, experimenting with selection, growing nostalgic for its past, dwelling pensively on its future.

Australians, of course, have relatively little recent experience of adversity. Defeat in the Perth Test of January 2008 was the first for more than half the team members and coach Tim Nielsen as well. When consecutive series defeats ensued against India and South Africa, that experience broadened a great deal. Peter Siddle's first Test, in Mohali, was a thumping; so was what must very nearly have been his last, in Perth, when his career looked in the balance.

The Australian response was to experiment. Indeed, while English cricket fans often look on Australia as the copyright holders on continuity of selection, the concept has been very much in abeyance in the post-Warne and McGrath age. In the last two years, Australia has been represented by thirty players in Test matches and thirty-two in one-day internationals—which is a lot of cricketers in a country whose domestic competition contains only six participating states.

In essence, Andrew Hilditch and his panel have been auditioning players for longer-term roles, trying and discarding some, blooding and recalling others. Ricky Ponting's team have lost some Test matches, a few badly, been pretty hopeless at Twenty20, sometimes embarrassingly, and certain issues remain unresolved; temporary fixes have been found in the matter of slow bowling and the opening partnership.

In that time the selectors have studied a lot of talent in challenging circumstances, and also a range of attitudes: Siddle's, for instance, has taken him a long way; Doug Bollinger's seems to have set him back. The result was that, by Headingley, Australia had arrived at a workable line-up: not the most talented team to wear the baggy green, and still susceptible to pressure and unfamiliar conditions, but a committed unit.

England, by contrast, have become like the old Australia, sticking to very similar line-ups, represented in the last two years by twenty-three players in Test cricket and twenty-five in one-day internationals. Like the old Australia in every respect but one, of course: results, which have remained mediocre.

So while Australia have learned quite a deal from their defeats, England haven't learned very much at all. Nor have they learned much this summer. Their bowlers getting lucky for a couple of sessions has obscured the fact that their batsmen have been repeatedly perpetrating the same mistakes. Now confusion has broken out at the belated discovery that the team is not very good, when it never really was.

Geoff Miller's lulling sentiment about not becoming a bad player overnight has a corollary: you don't become a good player by one or two useful performances. English cricketers are very often said to have arrived when they have really barely set off. Nor do you become a great Test all-rounder by turning up every so often, bowling the occasional penetrative spell, blasting the odd fifty, and assuming Christ-like poses.

Much of the overriding problem with English cricket, however, can be glimpsed in what we're living through: the particular, peculiar and utterly unproductive attitude to defeat. It has become a running gag on this tour that to mention the 2006–07 Ashes is a breach of politesse; you would sooner mention war to Germans. Yet defeat leaving England 1–1 this summer was greeted like the fall of Gordon at Khartoum, when it was not only not the end of the world, but not even the end of the series. Here, Vince Lombardi was surely right: 'The greatest accomplishment is not in never falling, but in rising again after you fall.'

16 AUGUST
ENGLAND

A House Divided

So Jonathan Trott is to make his Test debut at The Oval. More power to him. The good news is that The Oval is perceived as an English stronghold, the bad news that it isn't the best place to make one's Test debut. On the last-on, first-off principle, for example, Paul Parker, John Stephenson and Alan Wells failed, and never played again. Australians starting their careers there haven't prospered much either.

Mick Malone, Shaun Young and Dave Gilbert never got another chance against England after being capped there— Malone and Young, in fact, never reappeared in Tests. It seems all too easy, having come in at The Oval almost as an afterthought, to be consigned to a footnote later.

No Ramps? Well, you could see that coming. Yet the reasoning that making runs in Division 2 of the County Championship is not a preparation for playing Test cricket is meretricious. What county cricket of any description prepares one for, apart from playing more county cricket, is not screamingly obvious. And after all, the vast bulk of Ramprakash's first-class runs have been at the highest possible level in England. What does Surrey's temporary relegation matter?

Yes, there is a difference between first-class and Test cricket, but that applies everywhere, and arguably less so in England than in some other countries: one is likelier to face a bowler of international quality playing for a county than while representing a West Indian island or a New Zealand province. Discriminating against Division 2 cricketers simply because they are in Division 2 smacks of making them prisoners of circumstance. The experience of playing in a poorer team has its advantages: more chance to bat under pressure, more opportunity to bowl long spells, more necessity to really covet victory. It might even be considered a useful preparation for representing England in Test cricket.

19 AUGUST
FIFTH TEST

The Fix Isn't In—Yet

'Ashes Match Fix Probe' screams the poster for today's *Evening Standard*, fulfilling two criteria for competent headline writing: strict factual accuracy and disingenuous sensationalism. The ICC's Anti-Corruption Unit is investigating reports of an indeterminate conversation between a figure 'suspected of links to illegal bookmaking' and an unidentified Australian cricketer, who promptly reported the matter to the authorities. No information was exchanged, no inducement offered—it's hardly Meyer Wolfsheim.

But memories of the cupidity and venality of cricketers ten years ago do not take much to revive, and corruption has been a nagging fear since Twenty20 began to go forth and multiply a couple of years ago. A precondition of the moral lapses of Hansie Cronje and others was a surfeit of pointless, meaningless cricket: the spread of Twenty20 contains the seeds of a repeat of that phenomenon. The Indian Cricket League's reputation was as a hotbed of gambling, and even the IPL did not help its profile by rejecting the assistance of the ACU.

There's no reason to think that Test cricket has been compromised since the Condon report. The players seem well aware of their responsibilities, and also of the penalties, since the investigations into Marlon Samuels and Maurice

Odumbe. On the other hand, it's a pity administrators continue to stack the schedules so pointlessly and heedlessly. Seven one-day internationals between Australia and England after the Oval Test? Fifty-nine IPL matches in six weeks? What better means of creating the kind of jaded, disaffected automata who slipped into malpractice a decade ago? Sooner or later, I fear, a newspaper will publish a sensational headline that exactly suits a case both in circumstances and seriousness.

19 AUGUST
FIFTH TEST

A Delicate Balance

This morning's papers, following up yesterday's story, elaborate on the alarming if vague reports about an unnamed Australian player approached in a bar a month ago by a bookmaker of shady reputation: the kind of scenario familiar during cricket's moral meltdown a decade ago. Occasionally, though, and without any assistance from the dosh-for-declarations and wealth-for-weather folk, cricket comes up with situations almost too perfectly contrived to be true.

Australia and England come to the Fifth Test at The Oval with the series perfectly poised at 1–1. Australia need only a draw to retain the Ashes; England need a win to regain them. If Australia lose they slip to fourth on the ICC Test match rankings—a fall from grace that ranks in the plummet class.

Australia won hugely at Headingley, but England's Siegfried, Andrew Flintoff, is back for a final fling, having foreshadowed a month ago that this would be his last five-day international. He dominated the Oval Test four years ago with pace, power and will. Sounds like the perfect marketing recipe.

The parity of the scoreline, however, almost seems a little misleading. Australia seem to have timed their run nicely, disposing smoothly of the England Lions in Canterbury on the weekend, and with all players fit and mainly in form. Five of their batsmen are averaging more than 50 this summer, and their pacemen are striking every 28.11 runs and 48.83 deliveries. With some rain about over the next couple of days, they have even mooted an unchanged side, again eschewing a frontline spinner.

Ahead of what may be his final Test in this country, Ricky Ponting today almost glowed with confidence. The weather and potential for interruptions will please him as much as they vexed him four years ago, when Australia needed to win but were confounded by the gloom of the ides of September.

England, by contrast, have faded markedly since their win in the Second Test. Only two of their batsmen average more than 40, and their pace attack's vital statistics are 37 runs and 64.95 balls a wicket. Worse, their success has been concentrated in two second-day bursts in favourable conditions: six for 69 after tea at Lord's, seven for 77 before lunch at Edgbaston. Spinner Graeme Swann has been still more spasmodic, taking 4 for 87 in the second innings at Lord's, two wickets for 322 everywhere else.

England's selectors have finally tampered with a top order that has so far shown all the staying power of a reality television celebrity, phasing out Ravi Bopara in favour of Warwickshire's well-performed Jonathan Trott, whom his captain Andrew Strauss confirmed would tomorrow bat at number five. Strauss, however, remains the key wicket: England's only century maker of the series, their scene-setter as well as their taskmaster.

Flintoff bowled yesterday in the nets but not today, which is essentially the reason this will be his final Test bow, his every appearance having become 'subject to medical advice'. In his role as people's champion, he will be crucial to the atmosphere of the Test, the crowd's subdued behaviour at Headingley being not just a function of the events on the field.

His knee should not incommode him: there is no need now to pace himself or hold back. Yet that game four years ago aside, his record here is nothing special: 53 with the bat, but 33 with the ball, 11 wickets spread across four Tests. To excel, moreover, he will need to rise not above his physical indispositions but the ungovernable expectations surrounding his return. It's hard to see him being a conspicuous performer.

The ground today was picture perfect. The pitch looks sound, if dry, and the outfield will be red-hot, with the practice pitches cut from the wicket table. The Sydney Pardon press box at The Oval, at the Vauxhall Road End, is one of the best appointed in England, a far cry from the old, cramped and stifling quarters on the far side of the ground, where the front rows were baked by the afternoon sun.

The media's only cause for complaint is that, before every game, staff apply a coating of clouded plastic to its slanted panes, apparently to improve the players' viewing conditions, but leaving the occupants peering at the play through a glass darkly—one wag four years ago dubbed it the Stevie Wonder Centre.

As the appointed window monitors were busily ruining one of cricket's best views today, it was hard to ignore the sensation that something similar is happening in this series. The English Premier League season began on Saturday, entailing a total eclipse of the sports media: soccer, incongruously, played all day today on the televisions in the press box. With the Ashes on a knife edge, most papers this morning led their sport sections with either Arsenal's Champions League win against Celtic, or further reverberations from the Harlequins fiasco, rugby meets not-so-Grand Guignol.

The first four days of the Fifth Test are sold out, but its reverberations may not be felt far from The Oval, or beyond the television audience willing to pay through the nose for their Sky subscriptions. In contention here, then, are not merely the Ashes, but the credibility of cricket as an English spectator sport. To back the hosts after their disarray at Headingley, moreover, a gambler would need nerves of steel.

20 AUGUST

Day 1

England 1st innings 307–8 (SCJ Broad 26*, 85.3 overs)

Nothing would be more pleasing than to report a sumptuous feast of cricket at The Oval today, with the Ashes on a
knife edge at 1–1 in front of a capacity crowd. Test matches,
however, aren't always like that, and this was less a struggle
than a scrap, even all day without ever reaching great heights,
while plumbing the odd depth.

Two English batsmen passed fifty; neither converted, and
most others perished to poor shots. Australian bowlers delivered 17 no-balls and three wides, their lousy over rate worsened
by the treatment of a minor leg injury to Ian Bell, and batsmen's
constant pulling away because of distractions in the pavilion,
perhaps from Stephen Fry's vivid tie. There was also some
ham-handed wicketkeeping from Brad Haddin, whose dozen
byes brought his series total to 75. It was a day preparing the
way for other days rather than a day in its own right, for
the value of England's 8 for 307 appeared magnified by the
pitch, on which the ball was already observably penetrating
the top, offering turn and playing at varying heights.

At the time he elected to bat, Strauss, like the proverbial
man whose mother-in-law has just driven his new car over
a cliff, would have had mixed feelings: the pitch was probably at its best, but the sky was overcast and the flags stiff
with wind. With rain reported at Woking, the covers were

only waved from the square five minutes before start time. In the event, apart from a brief sprinkle that opened a few umbrellas and caused the lights to be switched on after forty minutes, it only rained boundaries, nineteen of them before lunch, as the ball, swinging barely at all, fairly resounded from the bat.

Australia obtained an early break with the wicket of Alastair Cook, squared up by a ball angled across him from Siddle, reducing his average in ten Ashes Tests to just over 27. England have had greater worries than Cook this summer, so a gift for inconspicuous failure has served him well. That brought Bell, who rather lacks that talent, for all the talents he has. That he is England's ersatz number three here, without a hundred in that position in thirty-one innings, is an indication of just how crummy are the alternatives. It was an opportunity he would hardly have expected earlier this summer when Ravi Bopara was the man in increasingly comfortable possession.

A competent Test batsman, Bell nonetheless resembles a Lego man in his stature and stiffness, and Australians have toyed with him for a dozen Tests. The 2005 Ashes series was as forgettable for him as it was memorable for everybody else, culminating here with no runs from eight balls, two of which dismissed him. His fifth ball today might have seen him off, too, Siddle grazing his forearm with a lifter that Asad Rauf judged to have missed the glove.

Johnson's angle and lift also posed Bell difficulties, his second ball striking the glove, the third deflecting from the shoulder of the bat to square leg for a streaky single. On a pitch with more pace, Bell's policy of defending rather than avoiding short deliveries might have provided more business for Johnson's leg gully. On a day of less luck, Katich at short leg might have telescoped his arm to collect an airy flick when Bell was 22.

Johnson was less effective to the left-handed Strauss, strangely reluctant to bowl short and drifting instead into his pads, where England's captain picked him off like low-hanging fruit. It was one of those days, in fact, where Strauss looked set to bat until the crack of doom, and his snick behind from an indeterminate defensive poke was as incongruous as Patrick Stewart dropping an 'h'.

That Hilfenhaus's front foot was revealed on replay to have transgressed by 6 inches will have added to Strauss's chagrin. Believers in karma would have been satisfied, remembering that umpire Billy Bowden refrained from giving Strauss lbw to Hilfenhaus to the first ball of the Headingley Test. That, though, was a matter of judgement; this was inexcusable inattention: Hilfenhaus hugged the front line tightly all day, and was called on five other occasions.

Strauss's fall further burdened Bell, who began looking like a batsman coming off a first-class hundred, which he is, rather than a limp double failure in his last Test, which he also is. He fanned three exquisite boundaries through point, and after lunch added the shot of the day, an on-drive that wormed its way between mid-on and midwicket, and seemed to gather pace on the way to the boundary.

Australia, nonetheless, were thriftier in the afternoon, partly by dint of maintaining a line wide of off stump—at times, in Johnson's case, very wide indeed. Hilfenhaus plugged away for fourteen overs either side of lunch, giving away less than 3 an over, Siddle for nine overs either side of tea, conceding just 11 runs in toto. Lily Allen was in the crowd, apparently tweeting about the tedium, and one sympathised: when Collingwood fell for the fifth time in eight innings this summer in the cordon or behind the wicket, England were idling, in a match they have to win.

As at Edgbaston, Bell seemed to enter a slightly trance-like state as his innings continued. Having raced to 60 from 82 balls, he dawdled 55 balls over his last 12 runs with only one boundary, never looking troubled, but never threatening to wrest the advantage, before dragging on his first ball after tea.

The initiation of South Africa's latest gift to English cricket, then, was a challenging one. Cape Town-born Jonathan Trott, after some introductory words by Cape Town-born Andy Flower, had been presented with his cap before play by Madras-born Nasser Hussain: a very English scene. He took guard now with considerable deliberation, surveying the field with commendable coolness.

Each Test batsman arrives differently. David Gower famously pulled his first ball for four; Marcus Trescothick sweated forty-five minutes over his first run. Trott was twenty minutes, 12 deliveries and some salty sledges from Ponting at silly point before working North through midwicket for a couple. One of those deliveries was a surprise 67 miles-per-hour bouncer from Australia's stand-in spinner—a batsman could go through an entire Test career without facing such a ball. Trott's first Test boundary, from his thirty-second ball, was punched classily through cover off Clark. North almost crept through his defences when Trott was 29, an inside edge just saving him; a tendency to play around his front leg might get him into trouble when the ball does a bit. But it took a quicksilver throw from Katich at bat-pad to dismiss him after two encouraging hours.

After tea, the choice Australian bowler was Johnson, who was back to scattering pearls among dross, but who continued his happy knack of taking useful wickets, hood-winking Prior with a slower ball and abbreviating Flintoff's farewell with a quicker, wider one. Siddle then became the highest wicket-taker in the series when he removed Swann with the day's last ball, and the crowd dispersed wondering if they had seen a good day for England, a good day for Australia or an ordinary day for cricket. One thing they almost certainly witnessed was the first stage of a result, which can't really be bad news for anyone.

21 AUGUST

Day 2

In the Sydney Pardon press box at The Oval this morning, with an hour to go before play, they are showing the Channel 5 highlights package. For some reason, the colour is turned down, with the result that Ricky Ponting is being interviewed in black and white, his faded baggy green a ghostly baggy grey; with the gasometer in the background, you half expect Len Hutton to appear next, fielding questions from Brian Johnston or Peter West. It somehow suits the feel of this match so far—a polite, middle-aged audience watching some polite, middle-aged cricket.

There are, however, already shades of 1953, when Australia went into the Test without a slow bowler, relying on Bill Johnston's left-arm variations, and England chose two local boys, Jim Laker and Tony Lock. When chunks flew from the pitch's crust during Alec Bedser's first over, Lindsay Hassett walked up the pitch to confide to his partner Arthur Morris. 'I can see who this pitch has been prepared for,' he griped. But by then it was too late. Without a specialist spinner, Australia were unable to retard England's fourth-innings chase, and England won their first Ashes series in twenty years.

Which is not to say that I foresee events repeating, although the parallels are instructive, and complaints about the pitch, such as those from my esteemed colleague Scyld Berry in today's *Daily Telegraph*, seem misplaced. Both teams have stared long and hard at this surface. It was open to both to choose an XI to suit the conditions; Ricky Ponting could very easily have won the toss and batted, in which case I fancy Australia would have batted somewhat better than England. Scyld seems to fancy some sort of deliberate malpractice: 'It is an abuse of the spirit of the game to tailor a pitch quite so blatantly.' But had the pitch been prepared according to some secret administrative fiat, one would have expected Panesar's inclusion alongside Swann. Scyld's theory depends, then, on believing that the ECB are capable of cocking up even a conspiracy.

Hmmm, on the other hand …

England 2nd innings 58–3 (AJ Strauss 32*, IJL Trott 8*, 28 overs)

The Ashes tradition was minted at The Oval 127 years ago in an Australian Test victory wrested from the jaws of defeat. Nothing short of a repetition will prevent England regaining the Ashes after an Australian collapse unusual in the annals of the game, let alone the events of this series.

After a solid start, and chiefly to two bowlers in Stuart Broad and Graeme Swann who had hardly threatened them all summer long, Australia lost eight for 72 in 24.4 overs. The resumption after lunch had been delayed fifty minutes by rain and murk, which the visitors must now wish had lasted all day, but which might just have freshened the dry surface slightly. When it lifted, Broad snared 4 for 8 in 21 quick, mainly full and swinging deliveries; Swann chimed in with 4 for 18 in 43 slow, teasing and turning off-breaks.

Each wicket was received with hosannas from an excited and faintly disbelieving crowd, who had arrived with the expectation of heaving a valedictory cheer for Andrew Flintoff, but who weren't fussy. At the close of a prolonged day, England led by 230 at stumps with seven second-innings wickets remaining, Strauss having piloted them through a few late anxieties.

England's last two wickets added 25 runs in as many

minutes on resumption, Anderson's curious duckless streak of fifty-four innings coming to an end, and Broad laying about him to some effect. But this was clearly to be an attritional day, as Australia's batsmen prodded the pitch as though trying to stifle embers. On 4, Watson survived two handy shouts for lbw, first to Anderson, then Flintoff. Flintoff shot Asad Rauf a quizzical glance, although not quite as quizzical as the glare Watson cast at the deliveries reaching Prior on the second bounce.

Yet how much the pitch had to do with Australia's later decline is debatable. At the end of the first day, Peter Siddle described it as 'a decent wicket' that 'became deader' as it 'flattened out', and even ignoring the natural predisposition of bowlers to see the world as a giant flat-track conspiracy, no batsman here encountered anything truly unplayable.

Certainly there was more bounce from the Pavilion End than the Vauxhall Road End, and the surface gave hints of being two-paced, but the emphasis was on the repeated rather than the unique: Watson simply was hit on the pads by a straight ball, as at Edgbaston and Headingley; Hussey propped forward, as also at Edgbaston and Headingley; and Ponting, the key, dragged on, as at Cardiff and Lord's. When Michael Clarke, taken at short midwicket at Lord's, then drove in the air to short cover, Australia had gone from 0 for 73 to 4 for 93 in what seemed the blink of an eye.

There was some bad luck for Australia to rue, and good luck for Swann to celebrate, Rauf failing to hear the inside edge onto North's pad, then imagining an inside edge onto Clark's—incorrect in both cases. The excellence, nonetheless, was excellent indeed, particularly Broad's slower, away-swinging yorker to dismiss the dangerous Haddin, and Prior's sticky-fingered snare after Johnson had wellied a couple of boundaries. The situation would have been still worse for Australia had Cook, soon after holding Katich there, held Siddle (4) at short leg. As it was, Siddle got a few brave blows away as if to prove his earlier point. These batsmen: always complaining!

One area in which Australia have certainly changed their views is selection. If the use of part-timers North and Katich for thirteen of the twenty-eight overs Australia bowled before stumps was not an expression of regret for the exclusion of Hauritz, it was nothing, even if the bowler with the keenest edge was Johnson, who caused both Bell and Collingwood to fend rather limply to Katich.

Australia took the field with two hours to go as a fairly bedraggled assembly; even their huddle looked a tad perfunctory. Wickets excited them, and England were thankful for the aplomb of Strauss, whose straight bat and relaxed body language advertised his growing confidence. For his own part, Ponting must have gnawed his nails back to the cuticle— there can be few consolations after such a day, heartbreaking considering his many months of hard work and the patient application his team has shown in clawing their way back to parity.

History, as observed, might encourage him. Billy Murdoch's Australians won here in 1882 by 7 runs, carried to victory by the self-belief of Fred Spofforth, abetted by the timidity of the home team. But history cuts both ways, for

Murdoch would later become the only Australian captain to twice lose series in England—the fate that may now await Ponting.

21 AUGUST
FIFTH TEST

Marathon Men

Twenty-five days. Quite long in a life; in cricket terms, it seems an eternity. Yet the sporting marathon of this Ashes may now hinge on two spells of bowling in London, separated by a month, assisted by the weather, against the run of play. And in an era where cricket is increasingly sold in sterilised, mass-marketed twenty-over packages, what's not to celebrate about that?

As at Lord's, there was little at The Oval today to suggest what impended. Australia's batsmen were applying themselves diligently after commendable bowling efforts: it looked like a repeat of the grinding scenario that so bored Lily Allen on Thursday. Then the wickets came, as thick and fast as you could Twitter them. At tea, Australia's dressing room must have been like a wake—and not one of those convivial Irish ones either.

This has been a series on which time has borne heavily, for it has involved two teams harbouring a lengthy list of frailties, doing their best to conceal them and to limit the damage as and when they have been revealed. All of

England's shortcomings were exhibited, in every department of the game, at Headingley. Australia's weaknesses, mainly against the moving ball, have been exposed less often but more ruinously.

The key weakness underlined today is one the Australians have done their best to avoid talking about, but now need to acknowledge: a deep and abiding dependence on their captain Ricky Ponting.

It was on his masterful 150 that Australia based their near total dominance of the First Test in Cardiff; it was his bristling 78 in the Fourth Test in Leeds that launched Australia on their way to overhauling England's first innings on the opening day. His failures at Lord's, at Edgbaston and here, however, have been like mines below Australia's waterline, setting the team on its beam ends.

Today, as in the first innings at Sophia Gardens and the second at Lord's, he dragged on, failing to get his back foot across and reaching for the ball, exacerbating the effect of a crooked downswing. He had broken his duck with a similar stroke, thick inside-edging past Prior's left glove to fine leg. but Broad was skilful enough to find the necessary line and length again.

Ponting is the most distinguished Australian batsman of his era, and an improving captain—it was pleasing to hear a suitable tribute from the crowd as he came in to bat today, in what might be his last Test in England. But his physique has absorbed a lot of punishment in the accumulation of that splendid record.

A disc in his spine now occasionally catches on a spur

on one of his vertebrae, part of the trouble being that he spends so much of his time crouched, in the field and at the crease. Last June in a one-day international in Grenada, he tore ligaments and damaged the sheath that keeps the main tendon in place in his right wrist, a tennis injury less common in cricketers that impairs him in playing the pull shot. They are not, strictly speaking, injuries, more battle scars, the impingements of sporting mortality.

Knowing this, the Australians have missed a trick. For all the excellence of Michael Clarke's batting in this series, the fact that he continues to fill the number five berth condemns him to dealing with circumstances rather than creating them. It has also tended to magnify the vulnerability of Mike Hussey, whose defence today resembled the Maginot line: aesthetically impressive, fundamentally flawed. The ball to which he played forward did nothing out of the ordinary. Hussey simply committed his front foot to the line of the ball and remained rooted to the spot. His Test average for the last year has been a meagre 31.

Simon Katich was the pick of the Australian batsmen, without much reason to celebrate his birthday but at least marking it. He scores in unusual zones, on-driving with a flex of the wrists, glancing fine, working it forward of square. He doesn't hurt or humiliate bowlers, but does perplex them about the ideal line, and doesn't yield, sucking pressure up with a little recuperative walk to leg between deliveries. To spin, however, he remains a thruster of the front pad, which Graeme Swann exploited successfully during his resourceful spell. Further umpiring gaffes ensued, in a series dogged by them, from Asad Rauf, but when catchers are round the bat and batsmen are defending grimly one hardly expects otherwise.

If Australia return home having left the Ashes behind, and they will now be almost impossibly hard-pressed to prevent it, the scoreline will confuse future critics. They have had the three greatest wicket-takers of the series and four of the five leading runscorers, with seven hundreds to England's one: man for man, they might even be considered to have the edge in total talent.

The summer of 2009 has been burdened throughout by comparisons with four years ago. And just as hearing 'Jerusalem' and 'Nessun Dorma' every damn day this summer has been enough to make you curse Blake and Puccini, Sky's custom of screening highlights of 2005 on every available pretext has been consistently unflattering to the live cricket in between. The closer parallel to Ponting's 2009 Australians may now be Lindsay Hassett's team of 1953, who drove England thrice to the brink of defeat without being able to finish them off, then lost at The Oval on that crumbling pitch for which they did not select a specialist spinner.

History, of course, never repeats exactly. In 1953, Australia were an ageing side that had failed to renew itself; fifty-six years later, they are a young side still getting their bearings. But as in that Coronation Year, the series was of twenty-five days' duration, some of it dull, some of it tense, in which a few spells turned out to be decisive, and the last men standing prevailed: Test cricket in excelsis.

Day 3

Australia 2nd innings 80–0 (SR Watson 31*, SM Katich 42*, 20 overs)

Another Ashes year, another Oval Test, another South African in English colours making Australia sweat. There haven't been as many parallels between the 2005 and 2009 Ashes as perhaps the marketers would have liked, but Jonathan Trott today offered one, emulating his bi-countryman Kevin Pietersen from four years ago with a hard, heady hundred.

Of course, the likeness between Pietersen's death-before-dishonour 158 then, and Trott's less-is-more 119 now, was only skin-deep: Pietersen was all adrenaline, Trott pure phlegm. Nor does this innings loom in quite the same way, helping to build a lead of 545 rather than saving a Test outright. Yet this was Trott's debut, in a Test to decide the Ashes, and on a pitch made yesterday to look like 22 yards of broken glass: a situation requiring nous, nerve and technique. 'They call it Test cricket for a reason' is one of Steve Waugh's oft-repeated mots. The trouble is that it's usually only invoked when batsmen are smashing bowlers to parts distant; what Trott took today was not just a chance to become an international cricketer, but an opportunity to show how good he is.

The day's first ball, from Siddle, darted away off the seam, passing Trott's outside edge, brushing his trouser pocket: a good delivery that might have brought a bad decision, for the Australians appealed with convincing spontaneity and unanimity. The second ball angled in, squared him up and dropped into space off the leading edge. In Strauss, however, Trott had a very good model of the philosophy of concerning oneself only with the next delivery, for England's captain continued his serene progress of the night before, taking no risks, playing rigidly straight, and wasting not a joule of energy until he hit four fours in 13 balls as lunch approached.

His rival Ponting looked rather more embattled, in the last over before lunch letting his face do the fielding at silly point, drawing blood surprisingly red rather than green and gold. Having had recourse to a helmet, he later took a blow to the ribs from Flintoff. He gave a grin, accepted a cheer, and might even have mused nostalgically about the days when he was only booed.

Trott, meanwhile, was even more impressively composed than on the first day. With a receding hairline, he appears older than his twenty-eight years, and he certainly bats older, with a forward press that makes it look like he can barely wait to get to grips with the bowling, and a still head that bends low over the ball: it stayed still even when a bouncer from Siddle deflected from his helmet for four leg byes. Like many accomplished batsmen, he also plays late, drawing power from the weight of his body; a comrade like Cook, whose weight is so poorly distributed, and who depends on his hands for the little power he has, could learn a lot from watching him.

Despite a businesslike demeanour, Trott has his mannerisms, including an eye-catching habit of bugging the umpire about the balls left in the over, as though keeping constant track of the game, and to maintain peak concentration only for so long as it is necessary. Nor does he waste effort on petty mind games. When Trott was 74, he pushed a ball down the pitch to Johnson, who hurled it back as though to catch the batsman out of ground he had never left—a bog-standard intimidation trick these days. Trott took a step to one side, declining to make eye contact. 'Oh purlease,' the gesture said. In other words, English cricket has acquired a ready-made Test batsman; how much it deserves him is another matter.

A further matter still is how much pressure he was under. Johnson, pick of the bowlers last night, didn't resume until today's thirty-eighth over, while Hilfenhaus bowled only two overs before tea. Having scorned to choose Hauritz here, Australia appeared to have undergone a total conversion to the cause of slow bowling. Marcus North toiled manfully, unchanged in the afternoon session from the Vauxhall Road End, having probably never expected to bowl so many overs in a Test match and perhaps hoping never to again. But he is not a spinner of the front rank and wouldn't pretend to be; with Katich and Clarke also pitching in, part-time spinners purveyed almost half the overs. As throughout the tour, meanwhile, short leg seemed too deep. Twice when he was 22, Trott offered catches that a 1980s bat-pad fielder would have swallowed; likewise when Swann was 12 did Katich's lunge fall just short. Katich actually did his day's best work at cover, throwing a fast-thinking but slow-moving Prior out with a direct hit.

While Australia's bowlers never gave in, it is a comment on something that having watched England claim six wickets bowled or lbw the day before, they did not obtain a single such scalp themselves: a wicket-to-wicket line was surely what this pitch required. Ponting, meanwhile, lacked a little inspiration, posting a deep square leg for much of the day, and a deep point for almost all of it, Swann taking the bait with reverse sweeps that should have been cheeky but were largely risk-free. That set Swann in motion for another perky innings, disarming in its orthodoxy, dismaying in its ease, a feast of drives on the up and over the top, taking particular toll of the second new ball until he tried to prove he could hook as well.

Swann's rapid progress, which followed some clunking blows from Flintoff and Broad, enabled Trott to build his innings by steady accretion: in the afternoon session, he made 33 of the 133 runs added. Only once he had reached his hundred, with a crisp boundary off his pads, did Trott really open his shoulders, with consecutive fours down the ground off Clark. The declaration with twenty-one overs remaining came as something of a surprise: one would have thought that every run deepened Australian immiseration. Likewise unexpected was the delay in the use of Broad until the fifteenth over and third change. Watson and Katich made the best of the circumstances, Watson still stumbling round his pads a little,

Katich as flinty as usual, with the knowledge that a couple of breaks would turn a day that was merely forgettable for Australia into a full-fledged disaster.

Seventy years ago, England might have made more than their 5 for 654 in the fourth innings of the Timeless Test at Kingsmead, but for inflexible steamer timetables. Yet no other team has done remotely as well as the Australians now must to retain the Ashes, a task their countrymen laconically call 'a big ask'. Mind you, as Trott demonstrated this afternoon, good players come up with big answers.

22 AUGUST
FIFTH TEST

Pitched Battle

News Ltd's Australian representatives here are in panting pursuit of Oval curator Bill Gordon, whom they call an 'eccentric recluse', apparently because he won't speak to them, even if it's not quite clear what he might gain from doing so. 'Gordon is likely to stay in hiding as the state of his pitch becomes even more of a talking point with the Ashes on the line,' they report. 'He is under heavy fire for producing a controversial pitch where balls were already going through the top of the surface after day one, bringing up explosions of dust and bouncing randomly.' The hapless groundsman is painted as a combination of Howard Hughes and Bert Lock, the Old Trafford retainer who prepared the pitch in

1956 on which Jim Laker made such mischief. The latter remained eternally thankful to Nasser—Gamal rather than Hussain—for engineering the Suez Crisis, thereby wiping the controversy about his surface from the front pages.

Nonetheless, this looks a little like a story that may answer itself. On the 'controversial pitch' today, almost 400 runs were scored. The odd ball kept low—Peter Siddle gave Matt Prior an amiable smile after one bounced twice on the way to the keeper after lunch. But nothing stayed down on the line of the stumps, and while clearly dusting up, the surface has not cracked. It's what players sometimes call a 'one brings three' pitch, insofar as batsmen are most vulnerable on coming in, but time spent in the middle is repaid.

Players, in fact, tending to be philosophical about these things, have so far shied even from criticism, let alone condemnation: North commented this evening that the pitch had not changed observably in the course of the third day's play. So why are we in the press so paranoid about pitches that do other than play straight up and down, and at even heights? Bowlers complain that cricket administrators are always batsmen. Might be time for journalists to fess up. Are we impartial arbiters of cricket, or just batsmen in disguise?

22 AUGUST
FIFTH TEST

Over It, Moonwise

Jonathan Trott today became the eighteenth batsman for England—even if he did kiss the three lions on doing so, it is still a little difficult to call him an 'Englishman'—to score a hundred on Test debut. He is the fourth in his own team, Andrew Strauss, Alastair Cook and Matt Prior having had the same exciting, unforgettable, hard-to-live-up-to experience.

At the press conference tonight, Trott also suggested he would be a snug fit with the culture:

> It's quite hard to describe now to be honest. I'll probably have to sit down and think about it and reflect on it ... Hopefully there will be a successful result for us and it will be even more special ... Obviously the selectors showed huge faith in me and I'm pleased to be able to reward them.

A 'to be honest', a 'sit down and think about it', a 'hopefully' and an 'obviously': why, the man's a prodigy, already a master of the most mind-deadening maxims in cricket's lexicon. Fortunately it was his bat that had earlier done the talking, and most eloquently. If he continues exuding such aplomb at the crease, he is welcome to as many cliches as he likes afterwards.

23 AUGUST

Day 4

Australia 2nd innings 348 (102.2 overs)

The Ashes, for a generation almost thought of as an Australian birthright, will have to become used to shared custody. When Mike Hussey's long, largely lone hand, 121 in five and a half hours, ended to a bat-pad chance at 5.48 p.m., Australia lost the Fifth Test at The Oval by 197 runs, the series 1–2, and possession of the trophy they recaptured only thirty months ago.

Never all that great in Ashes cricket, the difference between what is and what might have been has this summer been measurable in microns: a dropped catch here, a no-ball there, and at The Oval a coin toss, which delivered England an advantage they never ceded. The gap was widened today by the infinitesimal distances involved in two run outs, costing Australia their captain and vice-captain at a crucial stage.

After batting so skilfully on Saturday evening, Australia's openers struggled to regather themselves this morning, Stuart Broad bowling a testing wicket-to-wicket line and Graeme Swann extracting considerable turn, although it was a ball from the latter going on with the arm to which Katich padded up in the fourth over that gave England their first breakthrough. For the fourth time in five innings, Watson then fell lbw to a straight ball, chest on, head outside the line—not the position one expects an opener to get into, really, as, indeed, Watson still isn't quite.

Two scoreless batsmen could hardly have been a more propitious beginning for England. Ponting was determined to pull Broad, while Hussey, facing Swann, and surrounded by two slips, a silly point, a short cover and a short leg, took 13 tense deliveries to escape his pair with a jab into the off side. But for almost forty overs, both offered an object lesson in batting on this pitch, which required immense care, great concentration and a sense of humour, accepting that one would periodically be beaten, and learning to think past it. The smile that crossed Ponting's face when he played and missed at Broad after lunch was probably the broadest of the tour.

There is pressure on bowlers under such circumstances, too. As at Edgbaston, Swann sometimes tried too hard, Ponting driving him through cover from consecutive deliveries off the back foot, then the front, Hussey pulling successive boundaries to raise the hundred stand. While Harmison hit the deck hard, extracting as much lift as anyone during the game, the conditions offered few incentives to Anderson or Flintoff. With Australia 2 for 217, the last nine wickets had fallen in the span of 551 runs, making the popular licensed-to-kill pitch story of the last few days that bit more difficult to sustain.

Hussey chipped to mid-on, called promptly and set off. Ponting, however, was watching the ball, much as at Trent Bridge four years ago when fate and Gary Pratt interposed. He was still watching, transfixed, as the ball reached Andrew Flintoff at mid-on, and he was only fully underway from halfway through the run, Flintoff's clean gather and powerful side-arm throw beating him by a distance. Flintoff contributed little to his farewell Test, but here was evidence that his cricket is more than brute force and ignorance, for an overarm throw would almost certainly have gone over the stumps after bouncing on the hard pitch surface.

This brought to the crease Michael Clarke, in his batting prime and in the pink of form, although for his first three deliveries he looked surprised and a tad uncomfortable with Swann's turn. The fourth offered a glimpse of relief, a ball he could clip to leg, and on the pleasing sensation of a crisp connection he set off. All summer, Cook had stood beneath the lid at short leg to no obvious purpose, as ornamental as a bird-bath. Now he extended his left leg, and the ball deflected from his ankle to leg slip as Clarke turned to regain his ground. Strauss's underarm throw was swift and accurate, dislodging a single bail as the bat reached but did not quite cross the line.

All this happened in a fraction of the time it will have taken you to read that paragraph—so swift it almost eluded umpire Billy Bowden, who seemed a little loath to call for the third umpire. Finally, as he walked in to repair the stumps, he made the appropriate signal, which in Bowden's case is rather like the barrel girl on a quiz show making the shape of a microwave oven. A roar announced that Australia's best two batsmen had fallen for 3 runs in six deliveries.

When Prior stumped North smartly, the batsman stretched too far by an ambitious sweep, only the margin of victory seemed in dispute. But England is still short of making the excellent habitual—Collingwood grassed a regulation outside edge offered by Hussey (55) off Swann, and Onions dropped Haddin (14) at short midwicket off Anderson. Hussey now looked utterly rehabilitated, moving into the nineties with a perfect pull shot off Anderson's predictable loosener with the second new ball, through them with a cover drive from his salad days, and to his first hundred in twenty-eight innings with a like stroke. Haddin celebrated his escape with two demob-happy shovels over cover, then perished to a wretched shot, trying to clear the two fielders deep on the leg side on a turning pitch—a shot that, at last, savoured of defeat.

It was not long in coming: Australia's last five went quietly, for 21 runs in 46 deliveries. Cook took two catches, and Graeme Swann finished the match with 8 for 158, although Stuart Broad's first-innings 5 for 37 earned him the individual award. The celebrations were noisy but, compared to 2005, relatively brief. Perhaps the spectators grasped that it had been a close-run thing; perhaps they also concluded this was something they might even get used to.

23 AUGUST
RICKY PONTING

The Disappointed

'Reckon me Mum and Dad'll still talk to me. And me wife. But who else?' Thus Kim Hughes in 1981 after Ian Botham had prised the Ashes from Australia's grasp—and he was

right, being never quite forgiven. 'Whatever you do,' Ian
Chappell told Hughes's successor Allan Border, expressing
a time-honoured prime directive of Australian cricket, 'don't
lose to the Poms.'

Now that Ricky Ponting has done it twice, he is clearly
expecting a warm reception. Australians will have woken to
the news that not only are they no longer custodians of the
Ashes, but they are now supporters of the world's fourth-
ranked Test team. Awakenings don't come ruder.

Yet Ponting, the scars of his fielding misadventures carefully dressed, was also putting the best face on his team's
performance, saying that he was 'very proud of the whole
group'—and in this he was not wrong to be. Of the team
chosen, only Mitchell Johnson and Phillip Hughes have
performed stubbornly below expectations, and even Johnson
gave glimmers of his talent.

A bowling attack without a single Test match in England
between them has kept the home side to just two centuries.
A batting line-up in which only the captain had made a Test
century in this country generated eight, and will be much
better for the challenges tackled. An inexperienced team,
moreover, has learned a lot about the essence of team success,
and how it differs from individual accomplishment. For
there are lies, damned lies and then there are the batting and
bowling averages of the 2009 Ashes, which show Australia
to have had the top three wicket-takers and six of the top
seven runscorers.

For Ponting the individual, the series will also have been
formative. One suspects that, as it did for Warne, McGrath

and Gilchrist in 2005, defeat will probably prolong his career. It was striking last night to hear him speak so emphatically about his desire to play on, without obfuscating or pleading for time to reflect, into the Ashes of 2010–11, and perhaps even further. To make such a statement so unequivocally in the shadow of defeat bespeaks considerable determination. Ponting may have in mind the experience of Border, the husk of whose defeated team in 1986–87 became the nucleus of the side he led to a huge Ashes win twenty years ago.

Whatever the case, and whatever the reception, the reality is that the captaincy is his for as long as Ponting deigns it. For all his merits, Michael Clarke cannot captain Australia from number five; no other batsman remotely fits the bill at number three. The difference between Kim Hughes and Ponting is that the cap on Hughes never quite fitted, whereas the cap on Ponting's head is faded, battered, very proudly sported and universally respected.

24 AUGUST
ENGLAND

The Light on the Hill

All was quiet at the Grange Hotel in Tower Hill first thing this morning. No enraptured throng or flock of dolly birds awaited Andrew Strauss's Ashes-winning team; the players were abed, or abar; the media stood around basically interviewing one another.

Behind closed doors, the celebration was undoubtedly more raucous. Andrew Flintoff is probably in a position to face his imminent knee operation without an anaesthetic. But the subdued note struck was no bad thing, for England remain a modest team with much to be modest about—something, to his credit, that Strauss seems to grasp.

'When we were bad, we were very bad,' he acknowledged in victory. 'When we were good, we were good enough.' The Saatchis would have admired such crisp phrase-making. England were minutes and inches from going 1–0 behind in Cardiff, and were stuffed so completely at Headingley that it almost counted as two defeats.

In three sessions, bowling talent met ideal conditions: at Lord's, England took six for 69; at Edgbaston seven for 77; at The Oval eight for 72. Otherwise, only Flintoff on the last morning at Lord's rose above the circumstances, and the performance left him spent for the rest of the summer. England's top order, meanwhile, looked counterfeit without its Kevin Pietersen watermark. Vice-captain Alastair Cook, Ian Bell, Paul Collingwood and Ravi Bopara all averaged less than 30.

Perhaps the most intriguing is Bell. In mathematics, a bell curve describes the graphical depiction of data clustered around a mean. In cricket, an Ian Bell curve describes a tendency in scores to produce a Test average of 40 while nonetheless remaining largely devoid of character or authority.

It's a cliche to say that Bell is hugely skilled while lacking temperament. But executing a cover drive is not a skill—it is a proficiency. Innings are not static exercises in stroke production; they need to be organised. And at this, five years and nearly fifty Tests into his career, Bell remains a novice, a curiously passive batsman, with strokes to make a purist swoon, but so grooved in his own game as to sometimes seemingly forget the game he is playing.

Fortunately, the captain himself is in his batting prime—his game refined and rationalised, limits understood and explored, his 474 runs at 52.66 at the top of the order securing him the Compton–Miller Award previously won by Flintoff and Ponting. Like one of Napoleon's lucky marshals, too, he enjoyed good fortune: with the toss, with the umpires, with the pitches.

Above all, he radiates a priceless sangfroid in action. To watch him on the second evening at The Oval, hemmed in by fielders but enjoying the contest enough to smile, was to see a man in harmony with his task. His task now is clear: to do rather better as a custodian of the Ashes than the England of four years ago.

At the time, it soon became clear that England had geared themselves to beating Australia and … errrr … that was it. After going on their bus-riding bender, they learned there was a little more to cricket than a single series—a discovery that left them looking as confused as Kevin Pietersen on meeting Cherie Blair. They were duly humiliated in Australia.

Thus Strauss's comment on Sunday: 'Last time we had not won the Ashes for 18 years so it was a step into the unknown. To a few of us this time it is familiar. We have to be conscious that this is a stepping stone, not the end.' The next stepping stone is South Africa this winter; it will also be a considerable step up. No wonder nobody's getting carried away.

24 AUGUST
AUSTRALIA

TINA

It's a curious scoreline: 2–1. It looks and can be definitive. England won the Ashes of 2005 by such a margin, having been, session after session, every bit the better team. England 2, Warne 1 might have put the matter more succinctly.

England's 2–1 success four years later is a great deal less marked. One suspects that the teams could continue playing some months yet and still be hard to split. In the nine-Test series of which Lily Allen fantasised last week, the likeliest result would be 4–3, with the winner and loser far from clear.

No power on earth should have prevented Australia from winning the First Test at Sophia Gardens. That Monty Panesar and Jimmy Anderson did has seemed increasingly absurd. Ricky Ponting's critics are mainly opportunistic and captious, but his underuse of Ben Hilfenhaus, overuse of Marcus North and misuse of Mitchell Johnson on the last day are all decisions he has probably quietly revisited.

Johnson's blow-out on the first day of the Second Test at Lord's, meanwhile, must be one of the curliest conundrums to have faced an Australian captain. To bowl or not to bowl?

With injury to Nathan Hauritz, Ponting had not so much an attack as a defence, and actually did not do a bad job of marshalling it. But by the end of the second day Australia had fallen too far behind to make a game of it, valiantly though they fought.

In fact, if there are grounds for optimism in Australia's performances this summer, it is that they fought consistently, even if it was mainly their own inadequacies making this necessary. Their big second innings at Lord's, Edgbaston and The Oval evinced a character probably out of proportion to the available talent; England's rout at Headingley was the equivalent of a massacre, a suicide pact and a mass desertion combined. Individually, too, the Australian players will probably receive higher marks than their team. The anomaly of the team's statistical dominance should act as a challenge to them and a standing reproach to every statto.

No individual in his team was so fascinating as the captain himself, whose cricket and life have taken an unanticipated turn. He is essentially leading Allan Border's career in reverse, being born in the sunny uplands of abiding success, now plunging deeper into the valleys of diminished expectation. Ponting will rue misfortunes with the umpiring, and also with the coin, especially at The Oval, even if Headingley provided a choice example of the proverbial 'good toss to lose'. And while he will hate the thought, he has made a good loser this summer, quietly living up to the lofty sentiments about the 'spirit of cricket' for which he was earlier in the tour vilified.

Cricket Australia's chief executive James Sutherland has opined unprompted that it would be 'totally unfair' to sack Ponting, which is a little strange, seeing as it's hard to imagine that being on anyone's agenda, and might even act like one of those statements by the boards of football clubs that express their 'full support at the present time' for an unsuccessful coach.

Ponting, in fact, has Margaret Thatcher on his side, or at least the old Tory apophthegm: TINA. There Is No Alternative to him as leader, or indeed as number three. As for Michael Clarke, the position of an ambitious deputy in an unsuccessful side is a fascinatingly ambivalent one, and he has been so squeaky clean in his demeanour on this tour, and so excruciatingly dull in his public utterances, that it has been just a little cloying.

Yet much as he may covet higher honours, Clarke seems to understand that he is not quite ready; indeed, that the *Australian team* is not quite ready for a change so convulsive in a period when the surrounding change has already been so significant. The Australians will have a hard enough time in the next little while making sense of the scoreline 2–1—or, in their case, 1–2.

24 AUGUST
AUSTRALIA

Consistent Inconsistency

Glamorgan's Tony Cottey was once asked why he was so inconsistent. Cottey's reply was the only one possible: 'If I knew that, I wouldn't be.'

It is the unanswerable question, yet it is the quality that both captains craved during the Ashes of 2009, and the one that eluded both their teams. In fact, it is hard to remember a series involving England and Australia in which triumphs were so absolute and capitulations so abject.

It cannot be through lack of preparation. Arrive early at any Test match these days and you will witness preliminary rites longer and more elaborate than some Twenty20 games. This summer, both teams have been in such impressive pre-match form, with squads of up to thirty in sponsored gear, including players, support staff and supernumeraries, that the apparent contest in numerical strength has sometimes been almost as compelling as the cricket.

It cannot really be through constant selection brainstorms. Fourteen players played all five Tests, seven on each side, and such changes as there were over summer related chiefly to injury. After a period of considerable experimentation for the last year, Australia made only two form-related alterations in the series, despite wild fluctuations in performance.

Australia's first innings scores were as unpredictable as

throws of the dice—6 for 674, 215, 263, 445 and finally 160—while their bowlers and keepers conceded more than 200 runs in byes, no-balls and wides. Of England, a perennial degree of volatility is expected. But wasn't Australia the team that used to control the controllables, bowl the bowlables and eat the edibles?

Not anymore, apparently, although you wouldn't perhaps notice. Around every international cricket team these days there is incessant talk of 'processes'; the Australians are as bad, or as good, as anyone. Chesterton would have been suspicious. 'Vigorous organisms talk not about their processes but about their aims,' he noted. 'It is weakness that prompts talk of efficiency, sickness that promotes drive for health.'

One of the troubling aspects of this approach in the context of the current Australian team is its complication of the game, cricketers being encouraged to develop variations, new strokes, new deliveries when they should still be working on the reproducibility of their core skills and stock balls.

In Australia, the idea of 'learning the craft' of cricket at first-class level has gone by the board: the player is now simply to be developed by specialist coaching staff, with coaches handing out skills like so many Boy Scout badges, and domestic cricket a process merely of auditioning for higher honours.

In the case of fast bowlers, that is also partly because of an apprehension about overworking them too young. But it does mean that modern Australian players of, say, twenty-eight are in cricket terms much younger than they used to be. And what's the point of having the best slower ball in the world if you don't have the experience to tell you when to bowl it?

Worse, once players have graduated to international level, they begin playing even fewer games away from it. Consider Australia's three-prong pace attack this season: Ben Hilfenhaus, Mitchell Johnson and Peter Siddle. They now speak for a total of forty-six Tests but only seventy-six additional first-class games. Johnson's career, for example, consists of twenty-six Tests, twenty-eight other first-class matches, and fifty-five one-day internationals.

Australians pride themselves on picking their players young. Glenn McGrath was twenty-three, Shane Warne twenty-two. Yet what were they but advertisements for keeping cricket simple? The latest stage in the reinvention of Shane Watson as an opening batsman, by contrast, belies the years spent turning his bowling into a work in regress. During his most recent injury, for instance, Watson worked with Dennis Lillee and Troy Cooley on developing conventional swing. 'The things I've done technically are definitely going to help my bowling and give me an opportunity to swing the ball and not just angle the ball in like I have been previously,' he said. 'It will give me a few more things in my repertoire, so I'm very excited by it.'

If all Watson's talk of 'working on' this or that about his bowling had paid off, however, his repertoire would by now have more varieties than Abdul Qadir and be bowled at warp factor three. Yet his bowling at Edgbaston and the Oval was as odd and ungainly as a weightlifter trying to slip into a G-string.

Australia arguably look to their captain too much, but in this respect he is an exemplar, a batsman with a strikingly simple game. He drives, he pulls, he plays off the pads, and he is pedantic about these core skills. He doesn't really cut, and he's never been particularly comfortable with the sweep and slog-sweep.

His state teammate, Hilfenhaus, was easily the summer's most consistent Australian bowler, for his cricket is unadorned and unalloyed. He bowls an outswinger at good pace, but within himself, with the very occasional variation thrown in, and his accuracy is the better for it. There, then, is a start to answering that question posed of Tony Cottey: if you want to be a consistent performer, a good start is consistency of method.

24 AUGUST
UMPIRING

The Daily Moan

Neville Cardus once asked Donald Bradman if complaints about umpiring usually came from the losing side. Bradman set him straight: complaints *always* came from the losing side. The Australians have spoken softly this summer about the standard of the officiation, but thanks mainly to the ICC cosh of conduct. Privately, they are more than a little chagrined, and not without good reason.

The decision-making this summer, especially of Rudi Koertzen, who looked like he had won a competition to umpire a Test while still being unsure of what the sport concerned was, and to a lesser extent of Billy Bowden, Billy Doctrove and Asad Rauf, has been variable in quality at best, incomprehensible at worst. Ricky Ponting stayed on the right side of the ICC on Sunday by professing approval for the forthcoming introduction of a full-scale referral system. He shrank from saying he wished it could be retrospective. But for the umpiring at Lord's, which cost Australia the wickets of Ponting in the first innings and Mike Hussey and probably Phillip Hughes in the second, the visitors would have at least further neared their improbable victory target of 522.

By the Oval Test, there was a slightly martyred air to the Australians' responses to umpiring verdicts. Marcus North was good-natured enough to smile at a poor lbw call against him, although Stuart Clark left no doubt that he was either a strong advocate or a recent convert to the referral system. Shane Watson let a sense of persecution get the better of him, gesturing to his bat when given lbw for the fourth time in five innings: in fact, replays showed the decision to have been correct, the ball striking the bat but after the pad.

Opinions will differ about the exact cost of difficult decisions. Ponting had a point when he commented that in finely balanced series, umpiring decisions take on disproportionate significance. But while the two teams were well matched, the victories were actually very one-sided, which it could be argued had the opposite effect.

The other comment in circulation this summer has been how irritatingly mannered many international umpires have become: Koertzen with his slow-rising left arm, Doctrove with his cigar-store Indian inscrutability, Bowden with his general tomfoolery. Although not irritating, Asad Rauf certainly is distinctive. With his flowing locks at Headingley, he resembled a superannuated rock god; after a haircut before The Oval, he looked rather more like Tonto. Is it merely a coincidence that the best umpires in the world—Aleem Dar, who was excellent at Cardiff and Edgbaston; Simon Taufel; Mark Benson—are the least eye-catching?

Will the referral system be the panacea? It was noticeable at The Oval that on a pitch playing at two heights and cutting all sorts of capers, Hawk-Eye continued producing what seemed deceptively perfect parabolae.

Andrew Strauss, meanwhile, has commented with justification that cameras might be introducing doubt into the very low catches they are meant to clarify. We've griped a long time about umpires. It probably won't be long before we're moaning about technology.

24 AUGUST
TEST CRICKET

Going Down

It's official. According to the ICC's championship table, Australia is the world's fourth-ranked Test nation behind South Africa, India and Sri Lanka, and barely ahead of the country, England, that has just beaten it over the course of five Tests.

Feeling chastened? Quite possibly. So long have Australians luxuriated in the success of their cricket team that confirmation of recent decline is a moment for sober contemplation. Yet there is also something exciting about its possibilities. The World Test Championship has hardly captured the popular imagination in its six years, being a case of Australia, daylight and then the rest. And the fact of these rankings mattering as never before is extremely timely.

All round the world, Test cricket is under acute social, cultural and financial pressure. Five days is a whole working week, and we know how long these can seem. The advertising and television dollar is fleeing to Twenty20, cricket's newest, shortest and richest format, which can be over in half the time Michael Hussey batted so tenaciously on the last day at The Oval.

South Africa, a fine team well led, has a lot to recommend it as Test cricket's number one, but it has never drawn home crowds of any size. In India, Twenty20 omnipotent reigns, and where its television audience goes, money and prestige follow. A Test world in which Australia continued to exercise unipolar power would have offered steadily diminishing satisfactions.

This summer in England has been a cricket crossroads. The Ashes of 2009 followed closely two of cricket's hottest versions of its new variant: the IPL in South Africa and the Twenty20 World Championship in England. In fact, to so soon after be plunged into a five-Test series, cricket's most traditional and now almost obsolete format, felt a little like dressing in period costume for an activity of the Society for Creative Anachronism.

What ensued was not a vintage Ashes series. The teams were too weak and the Tests generally too one-sided. The advantage did not fluctuate; it swung back and forth like a wrecking ball, indicative of two teams at war with their frailties as much as with each other.

Yet they were genuine *tests*, of ability, adaptability, character, endurance. One saw cricketers in extremis: indulging in mass man-love one week, fit for trauma counselling the next; performing tasks requiring extraordinary patience and self-denial like Ricky Ponting's superfine 150 in Cardiff and Michael Clarke's sublime 136 at Lord's, then exhibiting blink-of-an-eye brilliance like the run outs executed from close to the bat by Andrew Strauss and Simon Katich at The Oval.

Some games have one or the other. No game apart from Test cricket has both to such an extent. It is still the most thorough and authentic interrogation of a cricketer's abilities: the full 360 degrees, rather than the 90 degrees of Twenty20, or the 180 degrees of the one-day international.

It is still the game, moreover, where we come to know the players best, from their on-field talents, their attitudes in action and repose, their mannerisms and musings. Andrew Flintoff at The Oval, as close to retired as one could be while still on a Test ground, was granted a last glimpse of the possible on the final day, his bazooka-like throw to demolish the stumps ahead of the Australian captain's run tinged with grandeur and melancholy.

The Australian captain himself, so familiar to us hoisting trophies and popping champagne corks, has also shown a different side of himself this year: desperate and driven, but dignified and fair-minded. He has not been lucky; he has never complained or made excuses; in his daily dealings with the press and public, he has been a model both of honesty and of tact.

Test cricket, nonetheless, needs further fortification. One of its main problems is addressed by the world championship table, but only partly. There is a natural desire for a definitive answer to the question of which is the best Test nation, and it would best be determined by head-to-head contest leading to a final. Test cricket proves again and again that it is not archaic. But the old systems of bilateral arrangements and rigid cycles are.

The last great quality of the Test match is its sheer complexity, how much it gives us to think and talk about—the what was, the what did and the what might have been. A properly structured world championship would enrich the Test experience still further.

SCORECARDS

FIRST TEST   Sophia Gardens, Cardiff, 8–12 July 2009
Toss   England, who chose to bat   **Match drawn**

England 1st innings			R	M	B	4	6
*AJ Strauss	c Clarke	b Johnson	30	90	60	4	0
AN Cook	c Hussey	b Hilfenhaus	10	31	25	0	0
RS Bopara	c Hughes	b Johnson	35	76	52	6	0
KP Pietersen	c Katich	b Hauritz	69	196	141	4	0
PD Collingwood	c †Haddin	b Hilfenhaus	64	150	145	6	0
†MJ Prior		b Siddle	56	99	62	6	0
A Flintoff		b Siddle	37	66	51	6	0
JM Anderson	c Hussey	b Hauritz	26	69	40	2	0
SCJ Broad		b Johnson	19	22	20	4	0
GP Swann		not out	47	54	40	6	0
MS Panesar	c Ponting	b Hauritz	4	15	17	0	0
EXTRAS	(b 13, lb 11, w 2, nb 12)		38				
TOTAL	(all out, 106.5 overs, 442 mins)		435				

FoW:
1-21	(Cook, 7.6 ov)		2-67	(Strauss, 19.6 ov)
3-90	(Bopara, 24.4 ov)		4-228	(Collingwood, 65.3 ov)
5-421	(Pietersen, 70.5 ov)		6-327	(Flintoff, 86.4 ov)
7-329	(Prior, 88.3 ov)		8-355	(Broad, 93.5 ov)
9-423	(Anderson, 102.4 ov)		10-435	(Panesar, 106.5 ov)

Bowling	O	M	R	W	
Johnson	22	2	87	3	
Hilfenhaus	27	5	77	2	(4nb, 1w)
Siddle	27	3	121	2	(5nb, 1w)
Hauritz	23.5	1	95	3	(3nb)
Clarke	5	0	20	0	
Katich	2	0	11	0	

Australia 1st innings			R	M	B	4	6
PJ Hughes	c †Prior	b Flintoff	36	61	54	5	0
SM Katich	lbw	b Anderson	122	325	261	12	0
*RT Ponting		b Panesar	150	313	224	14	1
MEK Hussey	c †Prior	b Anderson	3	24	16	0	0
MJ Clarke	c †Prior	b Broad	83	176	145	9	1
MJ North		not out	125	357	242	13	0
†BJ Haddin	c Bopara	b Collingwood	121	200	151	11	3
EXTRAS	(b 9, lb 14, w 4, nb 7)		34				
TOTAL	(6 wickets dec; 181 overs; 724 mins)		674				

FoW: 1-60 (Hughes, 14.6 ov) 2-299 (Katich, 84.6 ov)
      3-325 (Hussey, 90.1 ov) 4-331 (Ponting, 94.5 ov)
      5-474 (Clarke, 136.5 ov) 6-674 (Haddin, 180.6 ov)

Bowling	O	M	R	W	
JM Anderson	32	6	110	2	(1w)
SCJ Broad	32	6	129	1	(2w)
GP Swann	38	8	131	0	
A Flintoff	35	3	128	1	(7nb, 1w)
MS Panesar	35	4	115	1	
PD Collingwood	9	0	38	1	

England 2nd innings			R	M	B	4	6
*AJ Strauss	c †Haddin	b Hauritz	17	78	54	1	0
AN Cook	lbw	b Johnson	6	17	12	1	0
RS Bopara	lbw	b Hilfenhaus	1	4	3	0	0
KP Pietersen		b Hilfenhaus	8	20	24	0	0
PD Collingwood	c Hussey	b Siddle	74	344	245	6	0
†MJ Prior	c Clarke	b Hauritz	14	37	32	1	0
A Flintoff	c Ponting	b Johnson	26	89	71	3	0
SCJ Broad	lbw	b Hauritz	14	61	47	1	0
GP Swann	lbw	b Hilfenhaus	31	73	63	4	0
JM Anderson		not out	21	69	53	3	0
MS Panesar		not out	7	37	35	1	0
EXTRAS	(b 9, lb 9, w 4, nb 11)		33				
TOTAL	(9 wickets; 105 overs; 414 mins)		252				

FoW   1-13   (Cook, 4.3 ov)   2-17   (Bopara, 5.3 ov)
      3-31   (Pietersen, 10.4 ov)   4-46   (Strauss, 16.6 ov)
      5-70   (Prior, 26.3 ov)   6-127   (Flintoff, 49.4 ov)
      7-159   (Broad, 66.4 ov)   8-221   (Swann, 86.1 ov)
      9-233 (Collingwood, 93.3 ov)

Bowling	O	M	R	W	
Johnson	22	4	44	2	(1nb, 4w)
Hilfenhaus	15	3	47	3	(4nb)
Siddle	18	2	51	1	(2nb)
Hauritz	37	12	63	3	(2nb)
Clarke	3	0	8	0	
North	7	4	14	0	
Katich	3	0	7	0	

SECOND TEST Lord's, London, 16–20 July 2009
Toss England, who chose to bat **England** won by **115** runs

England 1st innings			R	M	B	4	6
*AJ Strauss		b Hilfenhaus	161	370	268	22	0
AN Cook	lbw	b Johnson	95	190	147	18	0
RS Bopara	lbw	b Hilfenhaus	18	20	19	4	0
KP Pietersen	c †Haddin	b Siddle	32	38	42	4	0
PD Collingwood	c Siddle	b Clarke	16	43	36	1	0
†MJ Prior		b Johnson	8	13	10	2	0
A Flintoff	c Ponting	b Hilfenhaus	4	16	10	1	0
SCJ Broad		b Hilfenhaus	16	50	26	2	0
GP Swann	c Ponting	b Siddle	4	6	6	1	0
JM Anderson	c Hussey	b Johnson	29	47	25	5	0
G Onions		not out	17	40	29	2	0
EXTRAS	(b 15, lb 2, nb 8)		25				
TOTAL	(all out; 101.4 overs; 425 mins)		425				

FoW: 1-196   (Cook, 47.5 ov)   2-222   (Bopara, 53.6 ov)
       3-267   (Pietersen, 65.1 ov)   4-302   (Collingwood, 76.3 ov)
       5-317   (Prior, 79.3 ov)   6-333   (Flintoff, 82.3 ov)
       7-364   (Strauss, 90.2 ov)   8-370   (Swann, 91.5 ov)
       9-378   (Broad, 92.6 ov)   10-425   (Anderson, 101.4 ov)

Bowling	O	M	R	W	
Hilfenhaus	31	12	103	4	(4nb)
Johnson	21.4	2	132	3	
Siddle	20	1	76	2	(4nb)
Hauritz	8.3	1	26	0	
North	16.3	2	59	0	
Clarke	4	1	12	1	

Australia 1st innings			R	M	B	4	6
PJ Hughes	c †Prior	b Anderson	4	10	9	1	0
SM Katich	c Broad	b Onions	48	141	93	6	0
*RT Ponting	c Strauss	b Anderson	2	19	15	0	0
MEK Hussey		b Flintoff	51	127	91	8	0
MJ Clarke	c Cook	b Anderson	1	21	12	0	0
MJ North		b Anderson	0	33	14	0	0
†BJ Haddin	c Cook	b Broad	28	28	38	3	0
MG Johnson	c Cook	b Broad	4	13	11	1	0
NM Hauritz	c Collingwood	b Onions	24	53	36	4	0
PM Siddle	c Strauss	b Onions	35	65	47	5	0
BW Hilfenhaus		not out	6	20	14	1	0
EXTRAS	(b 4, lb 6, nb 2)		12				
TOTAL	(all out; 63 overs; 267 mins)		215				

FoW: 1-4   (Hughes, 2.3 ov)   2-10   (Ponting, 6.6 ov)
      3-103   (Katich, 32.4 ov)   4-111   (Hussey, 35.6 ov)
      5-111   (Clarke, 36.3 ov)   6-139   (North, 42.3 ov)
      7-148   (Johnson, 45.5 ov)   8-152   (Haddin, 47.5 ov)
      9-196   (Hauritz, 58.3 ov)   10-215   (Siddle, 62.6 ov)

Bowling	O	M	R	W	
Anderson	21	5	55	4	
Flintoff	12	4	27	1	(2nb)
Broad	18	1	78	2	
Onions	11	1	41	3	
Swann	1	0	4	0	

England 2nd innings			R	M	B	4	6
*AJ Strauss	c Clarke	b Hauritz	32	64	48	4	0
AN Cook	lbw	b Hauritz	32	54	42	6	0
RS Bopara	c Katich	b Hauritz	27	136	93	4	0
KP Pietersen	c †Haddin	b Siddle	44	156	101	5	0
PD Collingwood	c †Haddin	b Siddle	54	121	80	4	0
†MJ Prior		run out (North)	61	50	42	9	0
A Flintoff		not out	30	34	27	4	0
SCJ Broad		not out	0	1	0	0	0
EXTRAS	(b 16, lb 9, w 1, nb 5)		31				
TOTAL	(6 wickets dec; 71.2 overs; 317 mins)		311				

FoW: 1-61 (Cook, 14.1 ov) 2-74 (Strauss, 16.2 ov)
      3-147 (Bopara, 44.4 ov) 4-174 (Pietersen, 51.1 ov)
      5-260 (Prior, 63.2 ov) 6-311 (Collingwood, 71.2 ov)

Bowling	O	M	R	W	
Hilfenhaus	19	5	59	0	(3nb)
Johnson	17	2	68	0	(1nb, 1w)
Siddle	15.2	4	64	2	
Hauritz	16	1	80	3	(1nb)
Clarke	4	0	15	0	

Australia 2nd innings (target: 522 runs)			R	M	B	4	6
PJ Hughes	c Strauss	b Flintoff	17	46	34	2	0
SM Katich	c Pietersen	b Flintoff	6	15	5	1	0
*RT Ponting		b Broad	38	88	69	6	0
MEK Hussey	c Collingwood	b Swann	27	100	63	3	0
MJ Clarke		b Swann	136	313	227	14	0
MJ North		b Swann	6	26	25	1	0
†BJ Haddin	c Collingwood	b Flintoff	80	187	130	10	0
MG Johnson		b Swann	63	94	75	9	0
NM Hauritz		b Flintoff	1	5	5	0	0
PM Siddle		b Flintoff	7	18	13	1	0
BW Hilfenhaus		not out	4	11	4	0	0
EXTRAS	(b 5, lb 8, nb 8)		21				
TOTAL	(all out; 107 overs; 459 mins)		406				

FoW: 1-17   (Katich, 3.1 ov)   2-34   (Hughes, 9.2 ov)
      3-78   (Ponting, 23.4 ov)   4-120   (Hussey, 32.4 ov)
      5-128   (North, 38.4 ov)   6-313   (Haddin, 87.4 ov)
      7-356   (Clarke, 98.2 ov)   8-363   (Hauritz, 99.4 ov)
      9-388   (Siddle, 103.6 ov)   10-406   (Johnson, 106.6 ov)

Bowling	O	M	R	W	
Anderson	21	4	86	0	
Flintoff	27	4	92	5	(8nb)
Onions	9	0	50	0	
Broad	16	3	49	1	
Swann	28	3	87	4	
Collingwood	6	1	29	0	

THIRD TEST Edgbaston, Birmingham, 30 July–3 August 2009
Toss Australia, who chose to bat **Match drawn**

Australia 1st innings			R	M	B	4	6
SR Watson	lbw	b Onions	**62**	130	106	10	0
SM Katich	lbw	b Swann	**46**	83	48	9	0
***RT Ponting**	c †Prior	b Onions	**38**	88	47	5	0
MEK Hussey		b Onions	**0**	1	1	0	0
MJ Clarke	lbw	b Anderson	**29**	94	55	4	0
MJ North	c †Prior	b Anderson	**12**	63	49	1	0
†GA Manou		b Anderson	**8**	20	11	2	0
MG Johnson	lbw	b Anderson	**0**	1	1	0	0
NM Hauritz		not out	**20**	78	50	1	0
PM Siddle	c †Prior	b Anderson	**13**	31	26	2	0
BW Hilfenhaus	c Swann	b Onions	**20**	37	31	4	0
EXTRAS	(b 5, lb 7, w 2, nb 1)		**15**				
TOTAL	(all out; 70.4 overs; 319 mins)		**263**				

FoW: 1-85   (Katich, 18.6 ov)   2-126   (Watson, 30.1 ov)
      3-126   (Hussey, 30.2 ov)   4-163   (Ponting, 38.3 ov)
      5-193   (Clarke, 49.4 ov)   6-202   (North, 51.4 ov)
      7-202   (Johnson, 51.5 ov)   8-203   (Manou, 53.5 ov)
      9-229   (Siddle, 61.5 ov)   10-263   (Hilfenhaus, 70.4 ov)

Bowling	O	M	R	W	
Anderson	24	7	80	5	
Flintoff	15	2	58	0	(1nb, 1w)
Onions	16.4	2	58	4	(1w)
Broad	13	2	51	0	
Swann	2	0	4	1	

England 1st innings			R	M	B	4	6
*AJ Strauss	c †Manou	b Hilfenhaus	69	178	134	11	0
AN Cook	c †Manou	b Siddle	0	7	4	0	0
RS Bopara		b Hilfenhaus	23	70	54	4	0
IR Bell	lbw	b Johnson	53	147	114	7	1
PD Collingwood	c Ponting	b Hilfenhaus	13	27	22	3	0
†MJ Prior	c sub (PJ Hughes)	b Siddle	41	100	59	6	0
A Flintoff	c Clarke	b Hauritz	74	116	79	10	1
SCJ Broad	c & b Siddle		55	92	64	9	0
GP Swann	c North	b Johnson	24	23	20	5	0
JM Anderson	c †Manou	b Hilfenhaus	1	7	6	0	0
G Onions		not out	2	20	14	0	0
EXTRAS	(b 2, lb 4, w 6, nb 9)		21				
TOTAL	(all out; 93.3 overs; 399 mins)		376				

FoW: 1-2   (Cook, 1.4 ov)   2-60   (Bopara, 19.2 ov)
      3-141   (Strauss, 44.1 ov)   4-159   (Collingwood, 50.5 ov)
      5-168   (Bell, 55.6 ov)   6-257   (Prior, 71.3 ov)
      7-309   (Flintoff, 80.4 ov)   8-348   (Swann, 87.3 ov)
      9-355   (Anderson, 88.6 ov)   10-376   (Broad, 93.3 ov)

Bowling	O	M	R	W	
Hilfenhaus	30	7	109	4	(4nb)
Siddle	21.3	3	89	3	(1w)
Hauritz	18	2	57	1	
Johnson	21	1	92	2	(5nb, 1w)
Watson	3	0	23	0	

Australia 2nd innings			R	M	B	4	6
SR Watson	c †Prior	b Anderson	53	183	114	9	0
SM Katich	c †Prior	b Onions	26	55	47	2	0
*RT Ponting		b Swann	5	6	7	0	0
MEK Hussey	c †Prior	b Broad	64	154	130	13	0
MJ Clarke		not out	103	281	192	14	0
MJ North	c Anderson	b Broad	96	208	159	15	0
†GA Manou		not out	13	39	28	1	0
EXTRAS	(b 4, lb 6, w 2, nb 3)		15				
TOTAL	(5 wickets; 112.2 overs; 466 mins)		375				

FoW: 1-47 (Katich, 13.2 ov) 2-52 (Ponting, 14.6 ov)
      3-137 (Watson, 43.6 ov) 4-161 (Hussey, 52.6 ov)
      5-346 (North, 103.1 ov)

Bowling	O	M	R	W	
Anderson	21	8	47	1	(1nb)
Flintoff	15	0	35	0	
Onions	19	3	74	1	(1w)
Swann	31	4	119	1	
Broad	16	2	38	2	(1w)
Bopara	8.2	1	44	0	(2nb)
Collingwood	2	0	8	0	

FOURTH TEST   Headingley, Leeds, 7–9 August 2009
Toss   England, who chose to bat   **Australia** won by an
innings and **80** runs

England 1st innings			R	M	B	4	6
*AJ Strauss	c North	b Siddle	3	16	17	0	0
AN Cook	c Clarke	b Clark	30	104	65	3	0
RS Bopara	c Hussey	b Hilfenhaus	1	10	6	0	0
IR Bell	c †Haddin	b Johnson	8	40	26	2	0
PD Collingwood	c Ponting	b Clark	0	13	5	0	0
†MJ Prior		not out	37	76	43	5	0
SCJ Broad	c Katich	b Clark	3	13	12	0	0
GP Swann	c Clarke	b Siddle	0	21	15	0	0
SJ Harmison	c †Haddin	b Siddle	0	8	6	0	0
JM Anderson	c †Haddin	b Siddle	3	7	10	0	0
G Onions	c Katich	b Siddle	0	1	1	0	0
EXTRAS	(b 5, lb 8, w 1, nb 3)		17				
TOTAL	(all out; 33.5 overs; 163 mins)		102				

FoW: 1-11   (Strauss, 3.6 ov)   2-16   (Bopara, 6.4 ov)
      3-39   (Bell, 15.3 ov)   4-42   (Collingwood, 18.3 ov)
      5-63   (Cook, 22.2 ov)   6-72   (Broad, 24.5 ov)
      7-92   (Swann, 29.4 ov)   8-98   (Harmison, 31.4 ov)
      9-102   (Anderson, 33.4 ov)   10-102   (Onions, 33.5 ov)

Bowling	O	M	R	W	
Hilfenhaus	7	0	20	1	(2nb)
Siddle	9.5	0	21	5	(1nb)
Johnson	7	0	30	1	(1w)
Clark	10	4	18	3	

Australia 1st innings			R	M	B	4	6
SR Watson	lbw	b Onions	51	121	67	9	0
SM Katich	c Bopara	b Harmison	0	9	4	0	0
*RT Ponting	lbw	b Broad	78	119	101	12	1
MEK Hussey	lbw	b Broad	10	16	10	2	0
MJ Clarke	lbw	b Onions	93	193	138	13	0
MJ North	c Anderson	b Broad	110	321	206	13	1
†BJ Haddin	c Bell	b Harmison	14	25	23	1	0
MG Johnson	c Bopara	b Broad	27	70	53	5	0
PM Siddle		b Broad	0	1	1	0	0
SR Clark		b Broad	32	24	22	1	3
BW Hilfenhaus		not out	0	6	3	0	0
EXTRAS	(b 9, lb 14, w 4, nb 3)		30				
TOTAL	(all out; 104.1 overs; 463 mins)		445				

FoW: 1-14 (Katich, 1.4 ov)   2-133 (Watson, 27.3 ov)
      3-140 (Ponting, 28.6 ov)   4-151 (Hussey, 30.3 ov)
      5-303 (Clarke, 72.6 ov)   6-323 (Haddin, 80.2 ov)
      7-393 (Johnson, 96.3 ov)   8-394 (Siddle, 96.6 ov)
      9-440 (Clark, 102.5 ov)   10-445 (North, 104.1 ov)

Bowling	O	M	R	W	
Anderson	18	3	89	0	(1w)
Harmison	23	4	98	2	(1w)
Onions	22	5	80	2	(2nb, 1w)
Broad	25.1	6	91	6	(1nb, 1w)
Swann	16	4	64	0	

England 2nd innings			R	M	B	4	6
*AJ Strauss	lbw	b Hilfenhaus	32	97	78	4	0
AN Cook	c †Haddin	b Johnson	30	136	84	4	0
RS Bopara	lbw	b Hilfenhaus	0	1	1	0	0
IR Bell	c Ponting	b Johnson	3	12	12	0	0
PD Collingwood	lbw	b Johnson	4	10	10	0	0
JM Anderson	c Ponting	b Hilfenhaus	4	20	10	1	0
†MJ Prior	c †Haddin	b Hilfenhaus	22	40	29	3	0
SCJ Broad	c Watson	b Siddle	61	95	49	10	0
GP Swann	c †Haddin	b Johnson	62	100	72	7	1
SJ Harmison		not out	19	43	28	4	0
G Onions		b Johnson	0	8	7	0	0
EXTRAS	(b 5, lb 5, w 5, nb 11)		26				
TOTAL	(all out; 61.3 overs; 275 mins)		263				

FoW: 1-58   (Strauss, 22.4 ov)   2-58   (Bopara, 22.5 ov)
      3-67   (Bell, 25.5 ov)   4-74   (Collingwood, 27.6 ov)
      5-78   (Cook, 29.6 ov)   6-86   (Anderson, 32.3 ov)
      7-120   (Prior, 38.6 ov)   8-228   (Broad, 51.3 ov)
      9-259   (Swann, 59.2 ov)   10-263   (Onions, 61.3 ov)

Bowling	O	M	R	W	
Hilfenhaus	19	2	60	4	(9nb)
Siddle	12	2	50	1	(1nb, 1w)
Clark	11	1	74	0	(1nb)
Johnson	19.3	3	69	5	

FIFTH TEST Kennington Oval, London, 20–23 August 2009
Toss England, who chose to bat **England** won by **197** runs

England 1st innings			R	M	B	4	6
*AJ Strauss	c †Haddin	b Hilfenhaus	55	128	101	11	0
AN Cook	c Ponting	b Siddle	10	19	12	2	0
IR Bell		b Siddle	72	222	137	10	0
PD Collingwood	c Hussey	b Siddle	24	89	65	3	0
IJL Trott	run out (Katich)		41	125	81	5	0
†MJ Prior	c Watson	b Johnson	18	57	33	2	0
A Flintoff	c †Haddin	b Johnson	7	21	19	1	0
SCJ Broad	c Ponting	b Hilfenhaus	37	89	69	5	0
GP Swann	c †Haddin	b Siddle	18	43	28	2	0
JM Anderson	lbw	b Hilfenhaus	0	5	6	0	0
SJ Harmison		not out	12	17	12	3	0
EXTRAS	(b 12, lb 5, w 3, nb 18)		38				
TOTAL	(all out; 90.5 overs; 414 mins)		332				

FoW: 1-12 (Cook, 5.3 ov) 2-114 (Strauss, 28.1 ov)
3-176 (Collingwood, 47.5 ov) 4-181 (Bell, 53.5 ov)
5-229 (Prior, 65.3 ov) 6-247 (Flintoff, 69.4 ov)
7-268 (Trott, 74.2 ov) 8-307 (Swann, 85.3 ov)
9-308 (Anderson, 86.6 ov) 10-332 (Broad, 90.5 ov)

Bowling	O	M	R	W	
Hilfenhaus	21.5	5	71	3	(5nb)
Siddle	21	6	75	4	(4nb)
Clark	14	5	41	0	
Johnson	15	0	69	2	(8nb, 3w)
North	14	3	33	0	(1nb)
Watson	5	0	26	0	

Australia 1st innings			R	M	B	4	6
SR Watson	lbw	b Broad	34	94	69	7	0
SM Katich	c Cook	b Swann	50	169	107	7	0
*RT Ponting		b Broad	8	20	15	1	0
MEK Hussey	lbw	b Broad	0	6	3	0	0
MJ Clarke	c Trott	b Broad	3	9	7	0	0
MJ North	lbw	b Swann	8	28	17	1	0
†BJ Haddin		b Broad	1	13	9	0	0
MG Johnson	c †Prior	b Swann	11	27	24	2	0
PM Siddle		not out	26	54	38	5	0
SR Clark	c Cook	b Swann	6	14	8	1	0
BW Hilfenhaus		b Flintoff	6	10	21	1	0
EXTRAS	(b 1, lb 5, nb 1)		7				
TOTAL	(all out; 52.5 overs; 226 mins)		160				

FoW:
1-73	(Watson, 22.6 ov)	2-85	(Ponting, 26.6 ov)
3-89	(Hussey, 28.3 ov)	4-93	(Clarke, 30.2 ov)
5-108	(North, 35.3 ov)	6-109	(Katich, 37.1 ov)
7-111	(Haddin, 38.4 ov)	8-131	(Johnson, 43.5 ov)
9-143	(Clark, 47.3 ov)	10-160	(Hilfenhaus, 52.5 ov)

Bowling	O	M	R	W	
Anderson	9	3	29	0	
Flintoff	13.5	4	35	1	
Swann	14	3	38	4	
Harmison	4	1	15	0	(1nb)
Broad	12	1	37	5	

England 2nd innings			R	M	B	4	6
*AJ Strauss	c Clarke	b North	75	226	191	8	0
AN Cook	c Clarke	b North	9	49	35	0	0
IR Bell	c Katich	b Johnson	4	13	7	1	0
PD Collingwood	c Katich	b Johnson	1	9	7	0	0
IJL Trott	c North	b Clark	119	331	193	12	0
†MJ Prior	run out (Katich)		4	16	9	1	0
A Flintoff	c Siddle	b North	22	24	18	4	0
SCJ Broad	c Ponting	b North	29	43	35	5	0
GP Swann	c †Haddin	b Hilfenhaus	63	57	55	9	0
JM Anderson		not out	15	34	29	2	0
EXTRAS	(b 1, lb 15, w 7, nb 9)		32				
TOTAL	(9 wickets dec; 95 overs; 408 mins)		373				

FoW:
1-27	(Cook, 12.3 ov)	2-34	(Bell, 15.4 ov)
3-39	(Collingwood, 17.3 ov)	4-157	(Strauss, 54.3 ov)
5-168	(Prior, 57.6 ov)	6-200	(Flintoff, 64.1 ov)
7-243	(Broad, 74.2 ov)	8-333	(Swann, 87.4 ov)
9-373	(Trott, 94.6 ov)		

Bowling	O	M	R	W	
Hilfenhaus	11	1	58	1	(4nb)
Siddle	17	3	69	0	(2w)
North	30	4	98	4	(1w)
Johnson	17	1	60	2	(5nb, 2w)
Katich	5	2	9	0	
Clark	12	2	43	1	
Clarke	3	0	20	0	

Australia 2nd innings (target: 546 runs)			R	M	B	4	6
SR Watson	lbw	b Broad	40	101	81	6	0
SM Katich	lbw	b Swann	43	98	68	7	0
*RT Ponting	run out (Flintoff)		66	157	103	10	0
MEK Hussey	c Cook	b Swann	121	328	263	14	0
MJ Clarke	run out (Strauss)		0	5	4	0	0
MJ North	st †Prior	b Swann	10	31	24	2	0
†BJ Haddin	c Strauss	b Swann	34	95	49	6	0
MG Johnson	c Collingwood	b Harmison	0	5	5	0	0
PM Siddle	c Flintoff	b Harmison	10	14	14	1	0
SR Clark	c Cook	b Harmison	0	1	1	0	0
BW Hilfenhaus		not out	4	10	8	1	0
EXTRAS	(b 7, lb 7, nb 6)		20				
TOTAL	(all out; 102.2 overs; 431 mins)		348				

FoW:
1-86	(Katich, 23.6 ov)	2-90	(Watson, 24.3 ov)
3-217	(Ponting, 63.6 ov)	4-220	(Clarke, 64.5 ov)
5-236	(North, 72.2 ov)	6-327	(Haddin, 94.4 ov)
7-327	(Johnson, 95.5 ov)	8-343	(Siddle, 99.4 ov)
9-343	(Clark, 99.5 ov)	10-348	(Hussey, 102.2 ov)

Bowling	O	M	R	W	
Anderson	12	2	46	0	(1nb)
Flintoff	11	1	42	0	(1nb)
Harmison	16	5	54	3	(4nb)
Swann	40.2	8	120	4	
Broad	22	4	71	1	
Collingwood	1	0	1	0	

Ashes 2009 Averages

	Mat	Inns	NO	Runs	HS	Ave	SR	100	50	0	4	6
Australia batting												
MJ Clarke	5	8	1	448	136	**64.00**	57.43	2	2	1	54	1
MJ North	5	8	1	367	125*	**52.42**	49.86	2	1	1	46	1
RT Ponting	5	8	0	385	150	**48.12**	66.26	1	2	0	48	2
SR Watson	3	5	0	240	62	**48.00**	54.91	0	3	0	41	0
BJ Haddin	4	6	0	278	121	**46.33**	69.50	1	1	0	31	3
SM Katich	5	8	0	341	122	**42.62**	53.87	1	1	1	44	0
MEK Hussey	5	8	0	276	121	**34.50**	47.83	1	2	2	40	0
NM Hauritz	3	3	1	45	24	**22.50**	49.45	0	0	0	5	0
GA Manou	1	2	1	21	13*	**21.00**	53.84	0	0	0	3	0
BW Hilfenhaus	5	6	4	40	20	**20.00**	49.38	0	0	0	7	0
PJ Hughes	2	3	0	57	36	**19.00**	58.76	0	0	0	8	0
PM Siddle	5	6	1	91	35	**18.20**	65.46	0	0	1	14	0
MG Johnson	5	6	0	105	63	**17.50**	62.13	0	1	2	17	0
SR Clark	2	3	0	38	32	**12.66**	122.58	0	0	1	2	3

Australia bowling and fielding											
	Mat	Inns	O	M	R	W	Ave	SR	5	10	Ct	St
BW Hilfenhaus	5	9	180.5	40	604	22	**27.45**	49.3	0	0	0	0
PM Siddle	5	9	161.4	24	616	20	**30.80**	48.5	1	0	3	0
NM Hauritz	3	5	103.2	17	321	10	**32.10**	62.0	0	0	0	0
MG Johnson	5	9	162.1	15	651	20	**32.55**	48.6	1	0	0	0
SR Clark	2	4	47.0	12	176	4	**44.00**	70.5	0	0	0	0
MJ North	5	4	67.3	13	204	4	**51.00**	101.2	0	0	3	0
MJ Clarke	5	5	19.0	1	75	1	**75.00**	114.0	0	0	8	0
SM Katich	5	3	10.0	2	27	0	–	–	0	0	6	0
SR Watson	3	2	8.0	0	49	0	–	–	0	0	2	0
BJ Haddin	4	–	–	–	–	–	–	–	–	–	15	0
PJ Hughes	2	–	–	–	–	–	–	–	–	–	1	0
MEK Hussey	5	–	–	–	–	–	–	–	–	–	6	0
GA Manou	1	–	–	–	–	–	–	–	–	–	3	0
RT Ponting	5	–	–	–	–	–	–	–	–	–	11	0

	Mat	Inns	NO	Runs	HS	Ave	SR	100	50	0	4	6
England batting												
IJL Trott	1	2	0	160	119	**80.00**	58.39	1	0	0	17	0
AJ Strauss	5	9	0	474	161	**52.66**	49.84	1	3	0	65	0
KP Pietersen	2	4	0	153	69	**38.25**	49.67	0	1	0	13	0
GP Swann	5	8	1	249	63	**35.57**	83.27	0	2	1	34	1
A Flintoff	4	7	1	200	74	**33.33**	72.72	0	1	0	29	1
MJ Prior	5	9	1	261	61	**32.62**	81.81	0	2	0	35	0
SJ Harmison	2	3	2	31	19*	**31.00**	67.39	0	0	1	7	0
SCJ Broad	5	9	1	234	61	**29.25**	72.67	0	2	0	36	0
IR Bell	3	5	0	140	72	**28.00**	47.29	0	2	0	20	1
PD Collingwood	5	9	0	250	74	**27.77**	40.65	0	3	1	23	0
AN Cook	5	9	0	222	95	**24.66**	52.11	0	1	1	34	0
JM Anderson	5	8	2	99	29	**16.50**	55.30	0	0	1	13	0
RS Bopara	4	7	0	105	35	**15.00**	46.05	0	0	1	18	0
MS Panesar	1	2	1	11	7*	**11.00**	21.15	0	0	0	1	0
G Onions	3	4	2	19	17*	**9.50**	37.25	0	0	2	2	0

England bowling and fielding											
	Mat	Inns	O	M	R	W	Ave	SR	5	10	Ct	St
SCJ Broad	5	8	154.1	25	544	18	**30.22**	51.3	2	0	1	0
G Onions	3	5	77.4	11	303	10	**30.30**	46.6	0	0	0	0
SJ Harmison	2	3	43.0	10	167	5	**33.40**	51.6	0	0	0	0
GP Swann	5	8	170.2	30	567	14	**40.50**	73.0	0	0	1	0
JM Anderson	5	8	158.0	38	542	12	**45.16**	79.0	1	0	2	0
A Flintoff	4	7	128.5	18	417	8	**52.12**	96.6	1	0	1	0
PD Collingwood	5	4	18.0	1	76	1	**76.00**	108.0	0	0	4	0
MS Panesar	1	1	35.0	4	115	1	**115.00**	210.0	0	0	0	0
RS Bopara	4	1	8.2	1	44	0	–	–	0	0	3	0
IR Bell	3	–	–	–	–	–	–	–	–	–	1	0
AN Cook	5	–	–	–	–	–	–	–	–	–	7	0
KP Pietersen	2	–	–	–	–	–	–	–	–	–	1	0
MJ Prior	5	–	–	–	–	–	–	–	–	–	11	1
AJ Strauss	5	–	–	–	–	–	–	–	–	–	4	0
IJL Trott	1	–	–	–	–	–	–	–	–	–	1	0

Length and distance conversions

1 inch	2.54 centimetres
1 foot	30 centimetres
1 yard	0.9 metres
1 mile	1.6 kilometres